SOCIAL
MEDIA

9 1 1

A HANDS-ON GUIDE TO BUILD
YOUR BRAND AND BUSINESS ONLINE

DINA LIMA

SOCIAL MEDIA 9-1-1

A Hands-On Guide to Build

Your Brand and Business Online

www.SocialMedia911Book.com

Published by Dina Lima

P.O. Box 2007

Hurst, TX 76053

ISBN-13: 978-1456525132

ISBN-10: 1456525131

Printed in the United States of America

For my husband, Nestor Lima, whose inspiration and love motivate me to maximize each moment of my life. And for my two little twitters (daughters), Gianna and Nathalia, for their constant tweets of wisdom, love, joy, and support.

Ten percent of author proceeds for this book will go to LIFE Outreach International's Water for LIFE outreach, a nonprofit organization working to not only deliver fresh, clean water with every well drilled, but also bring hope to people living in extreme poverty. I encourage you to join me in supporting this very worthwhile cause at www.LifeToday.org.

CONTENTS

ACKNOWLEDGEMENTS

I am very thankful to the special individuals whose feedback and support helped make this project a success.

Beverly Smirnis for her excellence in editing.

Leslie B. Akins for her invaluable input.

Carrie Ebben for editing and proofreading.

Tom Pryor for his feedback and business mentoring.

My two little twitters (daughters), Gianna and Nathalia, for their constant love and very honest opinion of my work!

Nestor Lima, my wonderful husband, for his love, support, and assistance.

And of course, to God, the Creator of the universe and my divine mentor, who endowed me with talents and abilities to share with others.

PREFACE

Now is the most exciting time to take full advantage of your online presence. You can strategically make the best use of popular social media tools such as Facebook, Twitter, and LinkedIn to accomplish several goals to include:

- Improve search engine optimization to generate leads with the most potential for converting into viable sales.

- Boost brand recognition.

- Be in the same location as current and future customers.

While this all sounds great, it is important to be realistic. To wrap your hands around social media as new technologies are developed and existing ones enhanced, there is much to be understood and accomplished. Because of the vast wealth of information available through hundreds of resources, you could read to the point of experiencing information overload. To help, my focus in this book is to answer the three most pressing questions that entrepreneurs and business owners have:

1. Where do I begin?
2. What tools should I be using for my business?
3. How much does it cost?

Keep in mind that social media is not a one-size-fits-all strategy. Since each business has distinct needs, my goal is to provide a practical approach to help you know vital details of the most popular tools and their functionalities, and what kind of investment these new online marketing approaches require. With this information, I can assist you in making informed decisions on employing the top technologies that make the most sense specific to you connecting with your customer base.

To show you the potential for using social media consider the following:

- The 500+ million Facebook fans and businesses produce more than 60 million status updates *per day* (Facebook.com).[1]

- Twitter experiences approximately 50 million tweets per day, which translates to an average of 600 tweets per second (Twitter.com).[2]

- According to the *2010 Social Media Marketing Industry Report*, 80.1% of businesses plan to increase current Facebook efforts while 85.4% of large businesses plan the same.[3]

- Three in four women online actively use blogs, message boards, and social networks on a daily basis, according to the *2010 Social Media Matters Study* conducted by BlogHer.com and iVillage.com.[4]

The information provided in Section One will help you digest what you need to know, what you need to do, and how to do it—one step at a time. I will paint the big picture of social media and share ideas for designing, developing, and maximizing a successful, *integrated* social media marketing strategy for your business.

The *Let's Get Practical* segments in various chapters of Section One will guide you through different activities, exercises, and thought processes. The best way to learn is to dive in and get your feet wet. After learning more about the various tools discussed, strategies for particular needs and the ability to engage with customers will be better understood.

In Section Two, the *Social Media 9-1-1 Quick Start-Up Guide* will walk you through processes for capitalizing on your social internet presence. Based on your online marketing program, you will have the ability to set up the most essential social medial tools that ultimately benefit a business of any size. You will also find information on how to access my complimentary *Mastering WordPress Toolkit* from my website.

Social media is expanding quickly and because of this, it is imperative to become students of this new marketing approach by employing technologies that make life easier, benefit businesses, and most importantly, help nurture relationships with past, present, and future customers.

As Eleanor Roosevelt once quoted, *"With the new day comes new strength and new thoughts."* My hope is that the information and tips provided in this book will inspire new strength and new thoughts as you embrace and play to your own beat within the social media landscape.

To Your Success,

Dina Lima

Social Media & Web Design Consultant, Speaker and Trainer

CEO, SocialExecs.com and TexasGreenSource.com

INTRODUCTION

"Social Media is about sociology and psychology more than technology."

Brian Solis, Principal of FutureWorks

The response to a four-day contest sponsored by GreenPeace.org held between June 28 and July 1, 2010 to rebrand BP, the company suffering worldwide embarrassment due to the oil spill in the Gulf of Mexico, was staggering—655,989 views and 1,926 submitted graphics.[1, 2]

Although this example is one of unfortunate Social Media-enabled PR, it speaks volumes to the influence of social media and the power it possesses in bonding people with similar interests, concerns, and feelings.

Social media is about connecting people and thanks to the internet, our world is linked more now than ever before. For forward-thinking small business leaders like you, sitting idle as new technologies are developed and existing technologies changed is simply not an option.

As a smart business owner, you are well aware that regardless of the product or service you offer, you are in the business of people. Therefore, it is essential that creative ways to enhance your product, improve your service, and remain engaged with your client base stay at the top of your list for an overall success strategy. The good news is that social media makes this connection instant, but also more dynamic, exciting, easy, and cost-effective.

Okay, so why should you get involved with the social media ballgame? More than likely, your customers use these technologies and unquestionably, you want to be part of the conversation. Social media has enhanced the way we communicate with people, taking it to an entirely new level of immediacy, transparency, and honesty.

People live in the now and want practical information to help with problem resolution today. Remember, you can offer the very answers that people use search engines to find.

For starters, you need to get to the basics by answering the following questions:

- After conducting a search for your personal and business names on Google.com, are you happy with the results?

- Do you believe the search results do justice to the quality of products and/or services that you offer?

- Is your expertise being represented appropriately on the web?

- Are the keywords (words people use in the search box) part of your web copy (content in your web pages and blog posts)?

- Are the comments and testimonials from satisfied customers that you have collected over the years available to someone instantly on your website?

- Do you have an active online presence on Facebook and Twitter?

- Are your LinkedIn personal and company profiles 100%

complete?

The information potential customers find, or do not find, plays a huge role in getting them to visit your website. However, this is just half the battle; the other half occurs once people visit your website.

Questions you need to consider after visitors have entered your website include:

- Are people finding what they were searching for?
- Is the information on your site *relevant* to their search?
- If your website "sticky" enough to keep visitors around?
- Does your web copy speak to your current and potential customers?
- Is your web copy styled for online readers?
- Does the content of your web copy speak the visitor's language *in context*?
- How strong is your call to action?
- Would your visitors know the next step to take?
- Are visitors to your website enticed to contact you?

SOCIAL NETWORKS

When you establish presence in high-traffic social networks, it is as though you have an online billboard that announces your whereabouts so people can find you easier. In addition, having an online presence in these networks is an indicator to people that your business is on the cutting edge of technology, whereby products and/or services offered are the best. Not having a social media presence sends a clear message of the opposite and makes it difficult for existing and current customers to find you.

Today, consumers expect to log onto any of the major social networks and locate the business of choice. Therefore, not staying current with trends puts you at great risk for falling behind the competition. After all, the way your company is branded in the mind of consumers is critical to business success.

By being a part of various social media outlets, you are immediately placed in a different category, at least from a consumer's viewpoint. Interestingly, even the massively successful company of Microsoft realizes the importance and value of staying up to date on trends, which is evident in their multiple Twitter accounts and Facebook fan pages created.

Innovation coupled with staying current with trends needs to be a part of your company culture. Just imagine the position Microsoft might be in today if it had failed to make continual updates to the Windows Operating System!

Regardless of company size or industry, serious businesses and professionals interested in remaining on the cutting edge in this fast-paced and high-tech world understand just how critical it is to stay current with technological trends.

EMOTIONAL CONNECTIONS

Social media tools and technologies help to extend and nurture your emotional connection with customers and business partners in an entirely new way. These provide a cost-effective and efficient way to attract more online visitors with potential for converting to bona fide sales. Today's internet-savvy consumers use the internet as the first option search for anything and everything they want to buy.

As a well informed business owner, you know the secret to your success is centered on customer relationships and excellence in service, as well as providing customers with a great product or service. Throughout the years of business operation, you have likely discovered ways of developing a genuine emotional connection with your customers by using relationship building strategies. Today, social media tools can accomplish the same goal but easier and in real time.

SOCIAL MEDIA MARKETING

As a business owner, why should you consider implementing social media into your marketing strategy? Simply put, you must go where the bees are if you want your share of honey.

Every day, your customers surf the internet, engage in conversations with like-minded consumers, and share findings. According to the *Nielsen Global Online Consumer Survey*, 90% of participants said they trust the opinions of personal acquaintances, while 70% trust consumer opinions posted online.[3] Hence, you want to be part of the discussion, better yet, you want ways to initiate communication and gather invaluable information about what your audience wants, likes, or dislikes. The goal is for you and your company to be the resource with answers that customers want.

For instance, how easy can prospective and current customers find you when your name, your company's name, or the product and/or service you offer are searched on Google? The truth is it depends on you. Fortunately, you have control over the success of a search and by learning how and implementing the appropriate steps, business will increase.

Without doubt, social media technologies have revolutionized the way in which businesses operate, an exciting change that will forever mark this time in history.

Within my book, you will be shown the top free social media tools and be provided with guidance for setting them up and using them as a means of enhancing your company's internet presence while allowing you to manage the company branding in a more efficient and effective manner.

These tools cost nothing out of pocket although there is the investment of time and effort in building your business' online brand. Of course, for any business time equals money. Therefore, to use the social medial tools there is a price. However, the funds required are already a part of your budget so once you have decided how to implement social media into your marketing mix some of the funds could be redirected into online marketing efforts. Many businesses actually report greater savings when the focus is switched to online marketing initiatives. In fact, eMarketer.com's research finds that online ad spending will surpass newspaper advertising. For 2010, online advertising was estimated at $25.7 billion. Per eMarketer, "That makes internet advertising second only to TV among measured media."[4]

Depending on availability, you may need to outsource or hire the right personnel to implement and manage your social media strategy. However, you will quickly discover how practical these technologies are and the incredible results they produce. In addition, you will learn that social media requires a specific strategy for maximizing benefits.

ENHANCING YOUR BRAND

Stacy DeBroff, founder and CEO of Mom Central explains, "Social media offers new opportunities to activate brand enthusiasm."[5] When customers view you as an expert based on the relationship that has been nurtured, their enthusiasm can be fanned by your brand.

As David Alston says, "Social media is not a media"[5] meaning that the objective is to listen, participate, and build relationships.

When current and potential customers see you as the "go-to

expert" because of your branding, you immediately win their trust, which generates loyal customers.

CUSTOMER SERVICE AND SOCIAL MEDIA

Social media provides an excellent way to improve customer service in a far more practical manner. Alston explains, "With the advent of Web 2.0, blogging, tweeting, and commenting have become far easier than looking up a phone number and waiting in a queue. Thankfully, a growing number of companies have realized this and are staffing up to assist customers on the channel they choose—the two-way channel called social media."[6]

SOCIAL COMMERCE

Facebook continues to awe both consumers and businesses by making the experience more functional, practical, and convenient without having to leave your preferred social network. The various applications available allow you not only to import your blogs from your website and your YouTube favorite videos into your fan page, but you are able to combine electronic commerce with the power of social networking where Facebookers can buy and checkout from within your page. Chapter One will show you some examples.

PLANNING YOUR STRATEGY

Social media marketing requires planning, but most importantly, management. As you will find in this book, tips on how to design and implement your social media marketing approach right away are provided. Once you've established them, focus on managing your social media presence.

As a business owner, the one thing that needs to be maximized more than anything else is your time. If your time is split between being a spouse, a parent, a business owner, an active community member, and any number of other roles, you probably appreciate simplicity! Automation systems that make management of your social media strategies far easier are also covered in this book.

A word on creating your plan: although planning is very important, don't get stuck in just planning. You can spend a lot of money on consultants and lots of hours designing a perfect social media plan in a Microsoft Word document and never get started, all while your competitors pass you by.

When interviewed by CBS News 60 Minutes, Facebook's founder, Mark Zuckerberg was asked if he knew that Facebook would become this huge popular social network. Mark replied that he and his college friends thought that "No way would we be the ones who were contributing to kind of leading the whole internet in this direction."[7]

Create a game plan but don't get stuck just planning. The key with social media is to try different strategies, and as you do, you'll find what works best for you and your audience. For example, if you post a question on your Facebook Wall to your fans and you don't get any responses, it does not mean that they're not listening. It just wasn't the question that persuaded them to respond. The solution: ask the question in a different way until you find what works. You're not the only one in these shoes! Well established businesses and entrepreneurs have done and are doing the same thing to find what works for them and their niche.

My desire is to help you grasp the big picture of social media and show you how the most popular social networks work together so you gain a better understanding as to the power of taking an integrated social media marketing approach and get in the game!

SECTION I – ABC'S OF SOCIAL MEDIA

"The polling of Internet users shows that friends' recommendations are the most reliable driver behind purchasing decisions. Right now, that market is largely untapped. Facebook and other social networks can allow that to happen."

Yuri Milner, Russian Social Media Investor

1 – THE SOCIAL MEDIA ERA

"A year ago, businesses were uncertain about social media. Now it's here to stay and companies are rapidly adopting social media marketing. Much like email and websites first empowered businesses, social media is the next marketing wave."

Michael A. Stelzner, Founder, Social Media Examiner

Social media is hot and getting hotter.

You may think, *"Why do I need to go through all this effort?"* The answer is simple—your competitors already are and with consumers being extremely active online users, you cannot afford to be left behind.

Social media refers to the collection of internet and mobile-based tools that enable you to share and discuss information among people. However, the definition offered by Brian Solis, principal of FutureWorks, puts it in perspective best.

Solis says, *"Social Media is about sociology and psychology more than technology."* Hence, it boils down to connecting and speaking with people online, preferably your target market.

With all new platforms there is a learning curve. At times, it may seem overwhelming or intimidating but once you get the hang of it, and start engaging with your fans and followers, and best of all begin enjoying great savings on your marketing dollars by using these free online tools, you could end up liking this new and dynamic world of online marketing!

The facts about social media demand our attention. Consider the following astounding statistics that reveal the growth of social media and the way in which businesses and people are using it.

INCREASED USE BY MARKETERS AND SMALL BUSINESSES

According to the *2010 Social Media Marketing Industry Report*:[1]

- At least 67% of businesses plan to increase the use of blogs, Facebook, video or YouTube, Twitter, and LinkedIn.

- Approximately 81% of all small businesses are much more likely to increase blogging activities.

- For marketers, blogs are the top area they plan to use to increase social media efforts.

- About 73% of marketers plan to increase YouTube and/or video marketing.

- Some 93% of marketers now use Twitter and 71% plan to increase their use of the network to further their marketing objectives.

- Of all large businesses, 85% plan to increase activities on Twitter.

- For all businesses, regardless of industry or size, 72.1% plan to increase the use of LinkedIn.

ADDITIONAL IMPORTANT DATA

The *Small Business Marketing Forecast 2010* reveals that 50% of small business owners use social media for lead generation, 45% use it to keep up with the industry, and 41% use it to monitor online conversations.[2]

ISITE Design's *2010 Web Strategy Report* indicates that 73.5% of companies surveyed plan to make social media a priority. Among other online initiatives, web analytics scored second with 60.5%, closely followed by user experience at 59.5%, and rich media at 49.5%.[3]

REPORTED BENEFITS OF SOCIAL MEDIA MARKETING

Respondents of the *2010 Social Media Marketing Industry Report* revealed the way in which social media efforts have been beneficial:

- 85% - Generated exposure for the business
- 63% - Increased traffic, subscriptions, and/or opt-in list
- 56% - Resulted in new business partnerships
- 54% - Assisted in raising search rankings
- 52% - Generated qualified leads
- 48% - Helped sell products and/or services
- 48% - Reduced overall marketing expenses

MOST COMMONLY USED SOCIAL MEDIA TOOLS

The *2010 Social Media Marketing Industry Report* also shows that Twitter, Facebook, LinkedIn, and blogs are the top four social media tools used by marketers, which rank as follows:

- Twitter - 88%
- Facebook - 87%

- LinkedIn - 78%

- Blogs - 70%

- YouTube and/or other Video - 46%

HIGH CONSUMER USAGE OF TWITTER

Twitter is a micro-blog tool used by millions of people daily. Twitter has experienced tremendous growth since its launch. This tool is also popular among consumers, professionals, and businesses worldwide, and has proven to be outstanding for personal and business branding.

According to comScore, nearly 75 million people from around the world visited Twitter.com in January 2010.[4]

Per Twitter.com, "Folks were tweeting 5,000 times a day in 2007. By 2008, numbers had increased to 300,000, and by 2009, daily tweets had reached 2.5 million. From 2009 to 2010, tweets grew 1,400% to a whopping 35 million per day. Today [As of February 22, 2010] we are seeing 50 million tweets were occurring daily, an average of 600 tweets per second."[5] Just imagine! And Twitter.com has the reports to prove it!

HIGH CONSUMER USAGE OF FACEBOOK

Facebook is considered the most popular social networking tool used by over 500 million people around the globe available in over 70 languages.[6] Consider for a few minutes the magnitude of the following statistics of Facebook.com, although this is not a full list because it would be too lengthy!

- More than 35 million users update their status each day.

- The average user spends an average of 55 minutes daily.

- More than 60 million status updates are posted each day.

- More than 5 billion pieces of content are shared each week to include web links, news stories, blog posts, notes, photo albums and the like.

Statistics relevant to businesses on Facebook are as follows:

- Facebook has more than 3 million active Pages.

- More than 1.5 million local businesses have active Pages on Facebook.

- More than 20 million people become fans of Pages each day.

- Over 5.1 billion fans have been created by Facebook Pages.

- The average user becomes a fan of four pages each month.

SOCIAL COMMERCE ON FACEBOOK

Due to Facebook's increased popularity making it the preferred social networking site for a large number of the world's population, it's a no brainer for e-commerce businesses to embed the shopping experience for their clients within their Facebook business pages.

Large companies that see this huge potential are tapping into this tremendous opportunity. Some great examples of businesses that allow consumers and fans to buy and checkout inside Facebook include is 1-800 Flowers (*http://apps.facebook.com/flowers-store*), Delta Airlines (*http://apps.facebook.com/deltaticketcounter*), Avon's Mark store (*http://apps.facebook.com/mark-store*), Brooks Brothers (*http://apps.facebook.com/brooksbrothers-store*). See Figures 1.1 and 1.2.

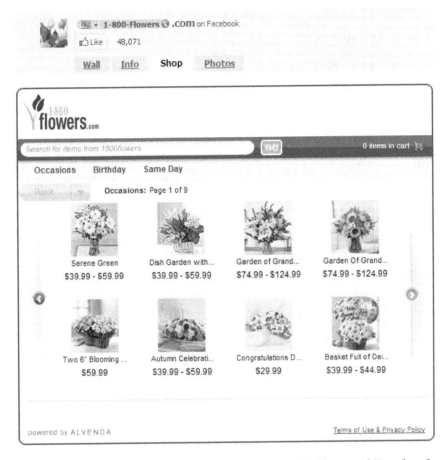

Figure 1.1 Order and pay for flowers on 1-800 Flowers' Facebook Fan Page

POPULARITY OF LINKEDIN FOR SMALL BUSINESSES

LinkedIn statistics should not be ignored. Every professional and small business owner would benefit from having a LinkedIn profile 100% complete. This profile is your image and therefore, completing it should be an essential step to boost both your company and personal brand. The following are the latest statistics for LinkedIn:[7]

- LinkedIn has over 70 million members in over 200 countries.

- One new member joins LinkedIn approximately every second, with about 50% of members being outside the United States.

- Executives from all Fortune 500 companies are LinkedIn members.

Figure 1.2 Book a trip on Delta's Facebook Fan Page

The numbers we have just seen are overwhelming and in fact, they seem almost unreal. However, one point is clear—social media is here to stay. For the small business owner who wants to continue growing his/her business and thrive in a highly competitive environment, a sound strategy to make social media a part of the marketing mix is imperative. I am thrilled that you're reading this book because the vast number of tips you'll receive will show you how to create your own strategy for success.

COMPARISONS BETWEEN SOCIAL MEDIA TOOLS

To run comparisons between different social media tools so you can view the latest metrics, visit *http://siteanalytics.compete.com.* In addition, to see a direct comparison between Twitter and Facebook, visit *http://siteanalytics.compete.com/twitter.com+ facebook.com.* For more direct links visit my website at *http://www.socialmedia911book.*

WHO USES SOCIAL MEDIA

Women

BlogHer.com and iVillage.com are the largest interactive communities of women online. Together, these websites conducted a study that quantifies and compares how different segments use social media, including gender, generational use, blogging focus, and media channel preference. The study also shows the way that different types of media such as blogs, social networks and online vs. offline media influence purchasing behavior. Some of the findings of the *2010 Social Media Matters Study*[8] are as follows:

- Blogs rank #2 as the preferred media source for product purchasing information, with internet search being #1.

- Approximately 59% use blogs to learn about new products and 20% use social networks.

- For 63% of the BlogHer network users, blogs are the go-to resource for making purchasing decisions while 37% use social networks.

- About 77% turn to blogs for information compared to 37% turning to social networks.

- Some 59% turn to blogs to find out about new products whereas 20% turn to social networks.

- For online adults who are active social media users, 73% use it more often than traditional media sources.

- BlogHer network users are significantly more active in blogs, Twitter, and Facebook than the average online woman.

- Of the 163.8 million people in the United States online, *87.1 million users are women!*

- Of the 126.9 million social media users in the United States, *67.5 million users are women* using social media at least once per week.

Needless to say, having a blog for your business is vital to remain connected with your audience, stand out in a crowded market, raise your rankings in organic searches, and increase revenue potential.

Baby Boomers

Of all social media websites, Facebook is the one preferred by baby boomers. As of January 4, 2009, the number of users for the 55+ audience was 954,680 but just one year later this number had increased dramatically to 9.763 million, delivering an increase of over 900% according to iStrategylabs.[9]

The eMarketer Digital Intelligence report, *Boomers and Social Media,* finds that baby boomers use social media for a number of reasons. For one thing, they expect technology to help them live longer and better lives. In addition, they anticipate social media will help them stay connected to family, friends, co-workers and, eventually, healthcare providers.

Lisa E. Phillips, eMarketer senior analyst and author of this new report, explains this mindset: "To fulfill these expectations, baby boomers are turning to social media where they maintain online social connections and make new connections. Online marketing messages that help them add people to their list of connections, while fostering online relationships is what baby boomers consider most important."[10]

Generations X, Y, Z, WWII

Facebook is at the top of the list of social media users for people in these segments. For Facebook.com, users are broken down by segment, as shown below by the eMarketer report.

- Generation X (Ages 27 to 43) – 76%

- Generation Y (Ages 17 to 27) – 65%

- Generation Z (Ages 12 and younger) – 61%

- WWII Generation (People from the World War II Era) – 90%

- Baby Boomers (Ages 44-62) – 73%

These statistics are mind-blowing but provide critical insight as to how different segments of the population are using social media. It is imperative for you as a business owner to know where your customers are online so that you can reach and connect with them effectively.

Getting Started

Start by becoming familiar with the various social media websites that your customers use and then start registering your company for those same sites. By knowing the different social networking tools that your target audience uses, you can create a useful social media strategy.

Although it seems like the whole universe is on Twitter and Facebook, it is essential that you know *your* audience. For instance, if the market buying your products and/or services is depending heavily on these technologies or others, it would be good practice to establish personal accounts on these same tools so you have the opportunity to connect with your clients, friends, colleagues, and business partners. This would be used as part of your business networking approach. As a business professional in today's society, it is expected that you at least establish presence on the top social networks.

1. For Facebook, log onto to your account. If you have not yet established an account, create one at *http://www.facebook.com*. You can follow the instructions provided in Chapter 12. Once logged on, conduct a name search on several of your customers. If you find a good majority of your top customers on Facebook, then you know that Facebook is a viable tool. Once your profile has been fully completed and a photograph uploaded, invite the customers and associates you found to be your friends. Also, invite your personal friends, colleagues, business partners, and people you meet during networking

events to connect as well.

2. For Twitter, log onto your account. As with the scenario above, if you do not have an account, visit *http://www.twitter.com* to complete the process. You can follow the instructions in Chapter 13. Enter as much information needed to complete the registration process. As before, conduct a search for your customers. If you find any of them using Twitter, this would be a good indicator that you too should have a presence on Twitter. At this point, you would need to go back to complete your profile and post several Tweets to the account prior to following people. With that, the chance that your customers, business associates, and other Twitter users will follow you in return is increased. However, if your Twitter account shows no activity, it could hinder people's decision to follow you. Consider customizing your Twitter background to include your company contact information, website and email address. This is a good practice for consistent company branding.

3. For LinkedIn, log onto your account at *http://www.linkedin.com*. If you don't already have an account established, follow the guidelines in Chapter 14. As a business professional it is essential to have your LinkedIn profile to connect with business associates, vendors, suppliers, other experts in your field, and even find quality employees and contractors.

2 – THE SIX STEP STRATEGY

"He who asks is a fool for five minutes, but he who does not ask remains a fool forever."
Chinese Proverb

Social media marketing goes beyond having a Facebook fan page and a Twitter account.

The secret to your success is in taking an *integrated* approach using various key tools and engaging with your target audience by providing them meaning and value through blog posts. This relationship brings invaluable information to you and your business because you discover areas needing more attention. You will also learn the things your customers really want. This research data is excellent for your organization, providing incredible insight as you work toward meeting and exceeding the needs of your customers but more importantly, staying one step ahead of their demands.

It would be great if social media brought overnight success but this is unrealistic. However, the tools involved will help speed up the process. Social media connects you and your market in real time and makes it possible to build the bond to keep customers coming back for more of what you have to offer.

Before getting into the technicalities of social media, it is necessary to set the foundation. For starters, a few steps need to be considered as you go through the process to create or fine tune your social media marketing plan.

STEP ONE – RESEARCH YOUR MARKET NICHE

Research results will reveal where you belong. In other words, your ability to identify the social media tools that your target audience is using will allow you to concentrate on those same technologies to best engage with them. Clarity about your target market will make your online marketing approach much more effective and position you to:

- focus marketing efforts strategically in attracting your client base.

- invest marketing dollars efficiently in reaching your ideal customers.

- become established as an expert in your market niche.

- stand out from the crowd in a saturated market.

If you are already in business, more than likely you have a customer database. You might consider conducting a survey of your clients to gather critical data. For this, be creative in your approach. Perhaps offer an incentive of some kind in exchange for information. You might also consider using online survey tools as a means of gauging your audience needs. Simply Google the keywords "free survey tools" to receive multiple choices.

Although this type of research may seem tedious and a bit overwhelming, your social media strategy might not render the desired results unless vital information is used to gain insight about your target audience. This would include their demographics, social media tools being used, ways in which customers are engaging, and where and what type of information is being searched to *drive* their purchasing decisions.

Initially, this research process is time-consuming but long-term, it will later save you not just time, but also energy and money. The results of your research will fine tune your efforts on the right kind of engagement that is needed with your audience, helping you put plans into place.

STEP TWO – STUDY YOUR COMPETITION

Although this might seem like a painful task, it is essential. You have to be aware of how others are playing the social media game and be open to making changes. Look at your competitors' websites, blogs, videos, Facebook pages, Flickr photo galleries, Twitter accounts, etc. Then, make a note of the things you are doing right and the appropriate steps you need to take to become more "socially-savvy" like the competition.

STEP THREE – CREATE A PLAN

The plan you develop will serve as a roadmap that tracks *where* you are going, *what* you will be doing, and *when* you plan to do it. From the research you completed, use the insight gained to create your social media marketing program.

Your plan should include a mission, vision, goals, timeframes, social media tools to be used, editorial calendar and a budget. Each goal should be broken down into tasks, which would then be assigned to specific individuals within your organization. Next, designate one person to manage each media channel, training them in the appropriate way of engaging with your audience. If your organization is comprised of only you, then plan your social media management into your schedule. Don't get distressed! There are several great tools that I will introduce to you in later chapters that will show you how to automate some of these administrative tasks.

Social media should be used to drive traffic to your website. So, when you have your site designed and built it should be a source of information specific to your market niche. Then, commit to posting a blog of new and innovative information on a regular basis. The content on your blog is what will drive people to your website. Focus on making your content informative, authentic and interesting. Good content provides value to your readers.

As a user of Facebook and Twitter, you do not control the rules of *their* game. The only thing you have control over is your website. Therefore, be sure to establish your website as a permanent base of information. As Mollie Elkman, an internet marketing expert, advises, "You have to get the traffic to your website, which you then convert into sales."[1]

STEP FOUR – ENGAGE WITH YOUR AUDIENCE

What does it really mean to be fully engaged with your audience? This means that you actively *listen* to them, which could be in the form of offering tips, expressing gratitude for your audience's comments and other feedback on your blog, having a Facebook fan page and Twitter account, or even providing a solution to a complaint specific to your company, product, and/or service.

When looking at home builders and the way in which they could engage fans and followers, Elkman suggests, "If a customer has decided to follow a 'friend,' or 'fan' your firm, they are interested in learning more about your company and the homes you build. To establish a stronger connection, start a conversation with them. Post photos of two completed kitchens, then, inquire of the two options, which one they like best. In fact, ask them to choose their favorite feature in their new home."[1]

This is what being fully engaged with your audience means and by doing so, you will experience exciting results from your efforts and also obtain invaluable feedback and insight regarding what your customers really want.

STEP FIVE – MONITOR RESULTS

Each business has its own needs and requirements, so its means of measuring results will also be unique. Decide the type of system you will use to monitor success or failure. For example, you may want to set target numbers for the following:

- Twitter followers.

- People re-tweeting your tweets.

- Facebook fans.

- Active conversations occurring per day, week, or even month.

- Hits receiving on your blog or website.

- Leads being gained from social media channels.

- New clients obtained from these efforts.

These examples are just a few of the various metrics you could use to evaluate your success.

STEP SIX – MANAGE YOUR REPUTATION

News spreads very quickly online and having happy customers who say the best things about you feels great! However, you will always have unhappy customers that no matter what you do cannot be pleased. While the goal is to have a database of happy customers, you should expect both positive and negative feedback.

Here are a few things to keep in mind when managing your

online reputation and branding:

Avoid Negative Comments

Don't be a ney-sayer yourself. Avoid making any negative comments. Stop to think how your business colleagues and customers would react to reading negative postings or feedback, but also the way your image would be affected. If you have any doubt, avoid saying it.

Maintain Your Professionalism

Never stoop below your position of leadership by allowing negative feedback to make you angry. Nothing good will ever come from this.

Offer the Best Customer Service

Always give good, old-fashioned customer service and make this part of your company culture. Remember, social media is an extension of customer relationship management. Therefore, if a customer makes negative comments, make contact directly to settle the issue. Once the issue is resolved, make sure that you bring closure to it on the medium in which it was generated.

Provide a Response Promptly

It is essential that you respond, not react. At all times, maintain composure.

Stay Away from Politics

Never get in the middle of business politics. This causes significant discord and results in broken business/customer relationships.

Be aware that many people are rude, insensitive, and simply do not care. These people show lack of respect to other people, both on and offline. Social media exposes the hearts of people, both good and evil. However, the law of sowing and reaping is still in effect, regardless of whether people believe they come from monkeys, or are divinely designed as unique individuals. As the saying goes, *"What goes around comes around."*

Businesses and professionals do not need to be dragged into unnecessary trouble within the social media sphere. Instead, this space should be utilized for the vast opportunities offered. Stay focused on one thing, *taking care of your customers.* Do this and your will have accomplished the best reputation management you could have.

Evaluate Your Search Engine-Friendliness

Search engines are great tools used for finding products, services, companies, and people. Use the following exercise to glean knowledge about where you are currently in terms of search engine-friendliness.

- Search for your name and company name using various search engines including Google, Yahoo, and Bing. Then, make a note of your findings and write down notes about where gaps exist between the things you would want your prospective and existing customers to see versus what is currently out there.

- Search for word variations that your target market might be using. For example, if looking for a florist shop, searches might be, "florist", "florist shop in Dallas", "organic florist shop in San Francisco".

- Click on the top five organic search results in return for your search (those that appear below the colored box when using Google.com) and make notes of the findings to include:

  o Is the page you landed on relevant to the terms or phrases (keywords) that were typed in the search box?

  o Is the content online reader-friendly?

  o Is there a clear call to action?

  o Are the social media buttons (i.e., Facebook, Twitter, and LinkedIn) visible on the website?

  o Does the website have a blog?

  o Can visitors comment on blog posts?

  o Is there a "tweet", "like" or "share" button, allowing visitors to share blog posts in other social networking platforms?

I just showed you how to research your competition painlessly! Observing what the competition is doing provides vital information so you can develop a better online marketing strategy than theirs. Remember, you do not need to reinvent the wheel, but by researching competitors you will begin to see opportunities and get started on the right track much quicker.

Go a step further:

- Search directly for the names of at least three of your competitors. Note what you discover about them and then make a list of things you see, including what they appear to be doing right (blogs, videos, photos, and presence on Facebook, Twitter, LinkedIn, Flickr, YouTube). Next, create a list of things that you need to start implementing to optimize your website, expand your online presence, and boost your own brand.

3 – OPTIMIZATION AND KEYWORDS

"Actions speak louder than words. Businesses must act. Once the door to social consciousness is opened, bring the spirit of your company through it to affect change."

Brian Solis, Principal at FutureWorks

There are various core elements that will help maximize your social media strategy so the results obtained are positive. In Chapters One and Two, I identified the need to take advantage of the power that social networking sites offer, such as Twitter, Facebook, and LinkedIn.

Optimization is the next item you will need to consider and for this, a list of keywords, the words people search by, needs to be identified. A discussion on optimization within this chapter will help you create this list of top-producing keywords to be used in your website content, including your blog posts.

In the following chapters, Chapters Four and Five, the discussion will be on websites and blogs, which are the places these keywords go to work for you, helping other people find your company when the internet is searched.

At the end of this chapter, I will touch on two other tactics, PR and

Pay-per-Click (PPC) campaigns that can be used when developing your social media strategy. With that information, you will begin to understand how one tool cooperates with and depends on the other tools. Opportunities to attract media attention are greater when everything needed is in place and the tools used are properly managed.

SEARCH ENGINE OPTIMIZATION

Search engine optimization is done for these reasons:

1. To rank higher in organic searches by providing relevant content.

2. To attract more readers by offering useful and intriguing information.

3. To draw media attention from news editors who are also interested in great content.

There are two kinds of optimization: on-page and off-page.

On-page optimization refers to the steps taken to optimize the content of each page or blog post on your website. Optimization is done for both search engines and users. In the following pages I will share with you the "how-to's" of on-page optimization.

Off-page optimization occurs when other websites link to your site. These are known as "inbound links." When other websites reference your site, they tell search engines to treat your site as a trusted and relevant source.

There are three factors to keep in mind when optimizing your website for search engines:

1. **Keywords**. In your content, speak the language of your users utilizing the keywords they use in their searches.

2. **Content**. Create compelling content for your users to establish your website as a viable and relevant source of information.

3. **Inbound links**. Get other websites to link to yours.

Bear in mind that inbound links are a result of doing your "on-page" optimization right. In the pages to follow, I will introduce you to various tools that will help you create premium content.

CONTENT IS KING

It is said that *"Content is king."* Here are several key reasons why:

- **Content is a magnet that attracts visitors.** If your content is interesting, visitors will read it. The goal of excellent content is to convert your visitors into customers eventually.

- **Content is loved by search engines.** Search engines want more keyword-rich content to index and store in their search databases. Keywords are the terms or phrases people use to search for things online.

- **Content influences other sites to link to yours.** These are your third-party endorsers, your word-of-mouth online marketers persuading others to check you out.

- **Content gains media attention.** Editors and reporters want content just as much as the search engines do. Great content such as research reports, white papers and how-to articles attract the media. Imagine getting exposure to their larger audience! It's important to have all your social media marketing systems in place so that you are prepared to benefit from this kind of publicity.

If you are creating a website, or if you need to bring your current website up to date, use a content management system (CMS) that has the blog component in it. This is discussed in detail in Chapter Six.

Some examples of CMS tools include WordPress, Joomla, Mambo, Drupal, which are among the most popular. These systems will let you add content to your website on a regular basis, helping your website rank higher in organic searches when you follow the keyword guidelines. Another benefit is that by having a blog embedded in your business website it will eliminate the need to maintain two sites, your corporate/business site and your blog site.

MAXIMIZE THE USE OF KEYWORDS

You want to use keywords to improve your organic searches by using words that users use to search. Keep a few things in mind about keywords:

- You are competing with other websites, not Google, so it is vital to come up with the right keywords to target your audience and continually expand them. Having these keywords help you draft your content to reach your audience.

- Use keywords in your page title tag, description tag, headlines, sub-headlines, body text, internal and external links.

- The more relevant keywords you use in your content, the higher you will rank on the search engine results page (SERP), and the more opportunities you will have to expand the potential market by getting more clickthroughs.

- You need to use search engine tools to know which keywords are being used by users when searching. These will save you a ton of time and make your research a lot more fun.

Use all kinds of keyword phrases in your web copy (your content):

- **Primary keywords**. The obvious terms that have a high

competition.

- **Related keywords.** The not so obvious terms that you may not have even thought of.

- **Long tail keywords.** These are longer keyword phrases.

- **Long tail keywords with questions.** Inquiry keyword phrases can help you tap into other market niches.

Primary Keywords

Primary keyword searches return the phrases that contain your keyword. You can use Google's free Search-based keyword tool *(http://www.google.com/sktool)* to begin building and expanding your list of primary keywords. This tool provides suggestions by words, phrases, websites or categories.

On Google's Search-based keyword tool main page, enter the website and the keywords you want to search (Figure 3.1).

There are various advanced search options with additional filters to narrow your search (Figure 3.2).

Google's search-based keyword tool will return the search results for the keyword phrases searched in the website you entered. You can search any website you wish—yours and that of your competitors. The results provide invaluable information for creating your list of keywords that you will want to optimize your website content, page by page.

The keyword search results will provide you the following information (see Figures 3.3 and 3.4):

- Keywords related to the website you're searching.

- Number of monthly searches for each keyword phrase.

- Level of competition for each keyword phrase.

- Suggested bid amount (for Google AdWords purposes); the greater the competition, the more the keyword phrase is worth.

- The page where the keyword phrase is mentioned in the website you're searching.

Website example.com

With words or phrases pots, pans

Tip: Use commas to separate terms or enter one per line.

Find keywords

Figure 3.1 Google's Search-based keyword tool main page

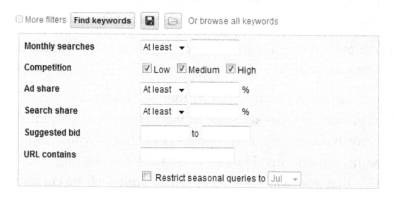

Figure 3.2 Advanced Search in Google's Search-based keyword tool

You can also take advantage of the export option to download your keywords into a Microsoft Excel spreadsheet for further analysis and sorting options (see Figure 3.5). Google is updating its Search-based keyword tool to include Google Adwords as noted in Figures 3.6 and 3.7.

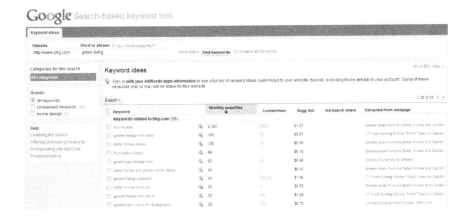

Figure 3.3 Google's Search-based keyword tool results

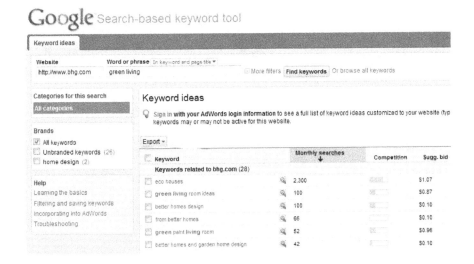

Figure 3.4 A closer look at Google's Search-based keyword tool search results

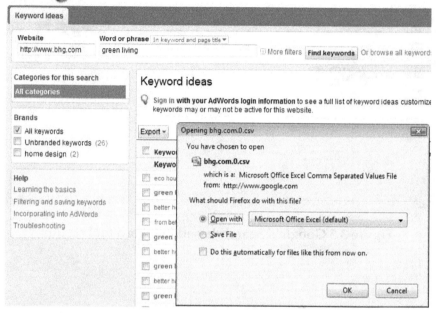

Figure 3.5 Google's Search-based keyword tool download function

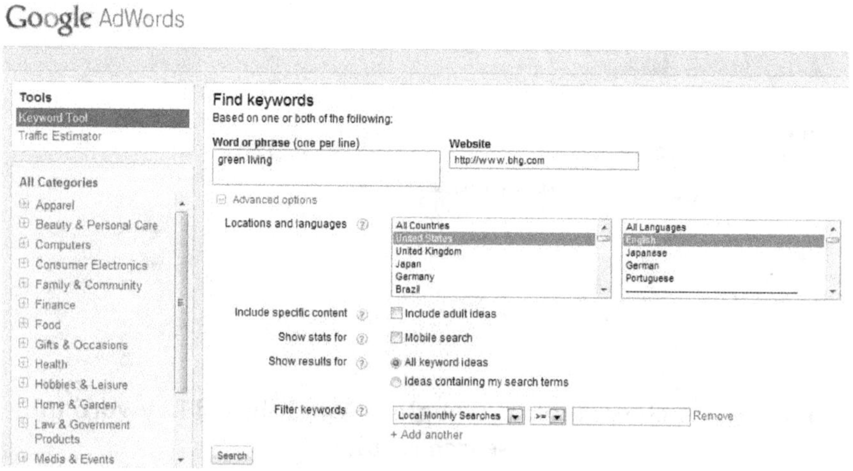

Figure 3.6 Google AdWords keyword tool with advanced search options

Keyword	Competition		Global Monthly Searches	Local Monthly Searches	Local Search Trends
Download ▼				Sorted by Relevance ▼	Columns
green living			74,000	40,500	
green living tips			2,900	1,900	
green homes			74,000	49,500	
green home building			6,600	5,400	
green building materials			8,100	5,400	
green living magazine			1,000	720	
green building			246,000	135,000	
green living ideas			1,300	880	

Figure 3.7 Google AdWords keyword tool search results

With the information provided by these tools, the guesswork of what phrases to include in your content is diminished. This makes writing your blog posts much easier, more focused and a lot more fun.

Remember, the goal is to make it easy for search engines to identify the page content and properly index your website. Search engines continually analyze and index websites to extract the best content (i.e., web pages, PDF files, videos) related to the internet searches. Their goal is to meet the needs of the internet audience by providing the most *relevant* results to their searches first. When you go through the effort to optimize the information for each page and blog post on your website, you will help the search engines meet their goals while they will help you achieve higher organic rankings.

Think of on-page optimization as a book. A book has a Title, a Subtitle, a Table of Contents and Chapters. Each chapter's content focuses and expounds on a specific theme. Follow the same idea when you optimize your web content. Therefore, for each page or blog post, the title, description, and content should focus on one theme. Sprinkle the keyword phrases throughout the content of the page that you want to optimize. Also, any hyperlinks that you reference on that page internally or to external websites should focus on the same idea. This helps the search engines detect easily what the content of the page is about and index it properly. Avoid using the infamous "click here" links. Instead, use keywords phrases in your hot links.

Now I will focus our attention on other kinds of keywords that can help you find other market niches.

Related Keywords

Don't make the mistake of using the primary keywords only. Related keywords help you broaden your keyword lists by including terms that may not have crossed your mind, but can help you attract these searchers. Let's take a look at another keyword search tool.

Wordtracker.com has a great related keywords tool. Suppose you sell some kind of music product and you want to find which words users are using when they search for the term "music". If you do a search on the word "music" you will get over one million results. By using the Related Keywords Tool, you'll tap into *other* words and phrases that could open other market niches for you and help you rank higher with search engines (see Figure 3.8). In the "music" example, *other* related keywords include "video", "bands", "internet radio", etc. (Figure 3.9). Access the free version of Wordtracker's keyword search tool at *http://freekeywords.wordtracker.com*.

Long Tail Keywords

Long tail keywords refer to longer keyword phrases specific to the product or service you sell and which people are using to find what it is that they are searching for.

Why should you care about long tail keywords? Long tail keywords represent a far greater number of searches than the "primary" or "head" keywords (i.e., "music", "realtor", "shoes").

Let's imagine you have a business that sells "hardwood floors." The long tail keyword search results from Wordtracker's free keyword suggestion tool are as follows (Figure 3.10):

"refinishing hardwood floors" (352 searches)

"distressed hardwood floors" (132 searches)

"exotic hardwood floors" (103 searches)

music 388,962 searches (top 100 only)	Want more *music* keywords?
Keyword	**Searches (?)**
1 music (search)	35,172
2 youtube music videos (search)	31,930
3 music downloads (search)	26,093
4 free music downloads (search)	17,084
5 free music (search)	13,675
6 music videos (search)	11,571
7 listen to music (search)	10,218
8 music lyrics (search)	9,659

Figure 3.8 Wordtracker's free keyword suggestion tool results for the keyword "music"

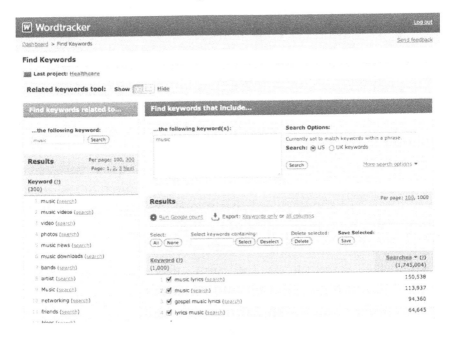

Figure 3.9 A Wordtracker Related keyword tool results

Remember that these are words people have used in their searches. By using these long tail keywords in your content, you not only optimize your website for the search engines, but you'll also tap into a group of people that know what they want, thereby expanding your market into other niches, represented in the lower number of searches.

The higher the number of searches on a particular keyword phrase, the higher the competition. Lower number of searches means lower competition.

hardwood floors 6,032 searches (top 100 only) Want more keywords?

Keyword	Searches (?)
1	hardwood floors (search)	698
2	bruce hardwood floors (search)	497
3	refinishing hardwood floors (search)	352
4	cleaning hardwood floors (search)	268
5	vinegar to clean hardwood floors (search)	241
6	how to clean hardwood floors (search)	197
7	repairing water damage to hardwood floors (search)	182
8	repairing water damaged hardwood floors (search)	180
9	how to refinish hardwood floors (search)	173
10	distressed hardwood floors (search)	132
11	exotic hardwood floors (search)	103
12	restoring hardwood floors (search)	85

Figure 3.10 Wordtracker's free keyword suggestion tool results for the keyword "hardwood floors"

Long Tail Keywords with Questions

Long tail keywords in the form of questions also present additional opportunities to tap into markets that know what they want. Based on our "hardwood floors" example, some of the question-style results returned in Wordtracker's free keyword tool are as follows:

"how to clean hardwood floors"

"how to install hardwood floors"

"how to design around hardwood floors"

"how to clean high gloss hardwood floors"

"how to keep hardwood floors clean of dog hair"

Some of the above examples can easily become titles to your blog posts. For instance, "How to Clean Hardwood Floors" is a keyword-rich title.

Your keyword research will provide hundreds and thousands of results. Select the keywords that fit best to attract your specific customer in a specific market and build your list.

Another great tool to consider using is Scribe, *http://scribeseo.com*. This tool is available for a monthly fee and is equipped with some great features to help you create amazing content.

By now you should have a greater understanding of how different kinds of keywords and keyword phrases play an important role in organizing and optimizing your web content.

The next two chapters will discuss how to get your website and blog ready and up to date. But before the general discussion on optimization and the role of keywords is concluded, I want to touch on other items you will want to consider.

ONLINE PUBLIC RELATIONS

Attracting editors and reporters to your website can be a huge benefit. This would result in bringing a massive number of visitors to your site through inbound links, not only from the sites doing the coverage but also from all other visitors who would comment. Your credibility will skyrocket when you obtain the endorsements from highly trafficked and trusted sources.

Increased inbound links will only come as a result of having optimized your content utilizing the on-page optimization strategies discussed in this chapter. This will help you build content that is authentic, interesting and adds value to your readers.

Imagine how your business would benefit from the exposure obtained via external high-traffic website links!

PAY-PER-CLICK (PPC) CAMPAIGN

Search engine optimization techniques increase your chances of appearing in organic searches that cost you nothing. Although these techniques take longer for you to see results because you have to create content around your keyword list, they are fundamental steps in your overall optimization strategy that will make your site more attractive to search engines, users, and the media.

But, is there a faster way to increase the traffic to your website? Sure there is, by using a pay-per-click campaign, PPC for short.

The PPC campaign will let you get results quicker. However, don't forget that the optimization steps discussed are still essential to your overall plan. Although your pay-per-click campaign can increase the amount of clickthroughs to your site a lot faster, if your content is not optimized for your visitors, they will not have a good enough reason to delve deeper on your web pages, let alone make the effort to contact you for further information, submit questions, or make a purchase! This will cause visitors to bounce off your website at the speed of light.

Once your visitors get to your site, have systems in place that will entice them to stay longer and persuade them to take action to contact you or buy on the spot.

THE POWER OF SYNERGY

The harmony generated when combining the various core elements of social media all help to drive more traffic to your website. Figure 3.11 illustrates this.

Search engines take notice when other people link to your website. This is viewed as a vote of confidence that will cause your page to rank higher because others have shown interest in it. The more people who share *your* links in the social media landscape, the more positive this will be for your website's overall rank results and credibility.

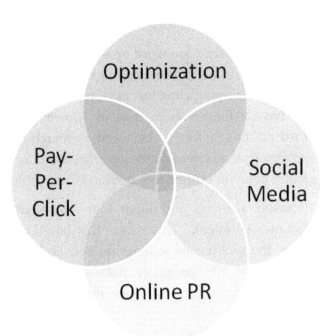

Figure 3.11 The Power of Synergy created by using a combination of various online marketing approaches

Steps for Optimization

The followings steps are designed to help you with your search engine and user content optimization, while increasing your organic search rankings.

1. Use Google's Search-based keyword tool to build your list of keywords and attract more visitors in your market niche. Access Google's keyword search tool at: *http://www.google.com/sktool.*

2. Use Wordtracker's keyword search tool to search for the same keywords and observe the results. For example, if you're in the remodeling business, type in "remodeling". If you have a flower shop, type in "flower shop." Access Wordtracker's free keyword search tool at: *http://freekeywords.wordtracker.com.* The paid option offers greater benefits, but the free version is an excellent start.

3. Microsoft also has a brilliant tool that measures users' "commercial intent." This means that based on the search query, the tool is able to measure *how likely* the user is to either gather information or make a purchase. The higher the percentage, the greater is the intention of the customer to make a purchase.

    Choose "Webpage (URL)" or "Query" to do your search. For websites, the tool gives additional information on "Transactional" and "Informational" percentages. Search the keyword phrases from your list gathered in the above steps to discover the *likelihood* of your market searching the web to either get information or to buy based on the keyword phrases they used to search. See Figures 3.12 and 3.13. Access the tool at:

http://adlab.msn.com/Online-Commercial-Intention/Default.aspx

4. Draft your web copy following the keyword guidelines presented in this chapter.

5. Open your social networking accounts in the top social media tools—Facebook, Twitter, and LinkedIn. You can follow the step-by-step guidelines provided in Chapters Twelve through Fourteen.

6. Link to other high-traffic sites you discover from within your industry.

7. Seize opportunities to contribute content to other websites that could help increase inbound links to your site. Provide feedback in forums. Add comments in other blogs.

8. Continuously expand your keyword list and use it when writing new content.

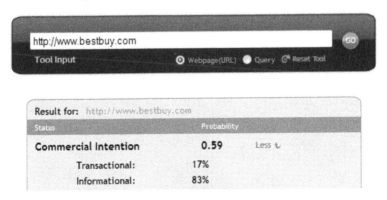

Figure 3.12 Example of a commercial intention percentage on a "Webpage (URL)" search in Microsoft's audience intelligence tool

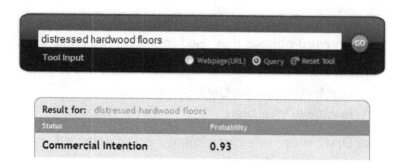

Figure 3.13 Example of a commercial intention percentage on a "Query" keyword phrase search in Microsoft's audience intelligence tool

4 – THE WEB 2.0 ADVANTAGE

"Innovation needs to be part of your culture. Consumers are transforming faster than we are, and if we don't catch up, we're in trouble."

Ian Schafer, CEO of Deep Focus

Since a primary goal of social media is to engage your target audience and drive traffic back to your website, now is the time to evaluate it. Your website is a living organism of your business. It is your storefront image on the web and your best, most cost-effective marketing tool if used appropriately.

Your website should be attractive yet simple for users to navigate and enjoy a positive and memorable experience. You can have a very pretty website, but it's not worth anything if it is not effective, and most importantly, if it's content is not relevant to the keyword searches that are leading visitors to your pages. It is fundamental for your website to be the point of contact for visitors to contact you, make a purchase, and engage with you.

If your website is old and really needs a facelift, then invest in polishing your online image. Your branding is very important and you cannot afford for your online presence to reflect poorly on your business and depreciate the quality products and great customer service that you already provide.

COMMON WEBSITE QUESTIONS

Following are the most common questions I get asked from business owners:

1. **I have a website for my business already and I'm happy with the design. I want to incorporate social media into my online marketing plan. What is the first step I need to take and what else do I need to do?**

    First, build a Blog site that mirrors the look and feel of your company website. Link the two to reference each other. You can have the Blog component embedded on your website, or have it separately. Use a content management tool such as WordPress. This will give you the opportunity to control your content by logging on to the administrative tool, and adding new content on a regular basis without programming intervention. As discussed in Chapter Three, content is king. Having a blog will enable you to exercise this vital business activity that today's internet-savvy consumers have come to expect.

    Second, establish or enhance your presence in the most popular social networking sites (Facebook, Twitter, and LinkedIn), and include these links in your company and blog sites. Promote these in your collateral printed material and email signature.

2. **My website needs a facelift. Where do I begin?**

    If you don't already have a logo or it's outdated, accomplish this first to help build your branding around it. Next, build your website using a content management tool such as WordPress, Joomla, or other. If you love simplicity and user-friendliness, choose WordPress. There are thousands of free and premium templates that can be customized easily. If you're not technically inclined, you may need to hire a programmer to help you with the customization aspect, but the investment is well worth it.

Whether you want to manage the social media marketing aspect of your business yourself, or are thinking of outsourcing it, hire an expert web designer that knows SEO, understands social media, and can train you on how to administer your website. A consultant with a varied skill set will be most beneficial to you.

3. **How much does having website or blog site built cost?**

This really will depend on the particular needs of your business and the kind of website you require (i.e., e-commerce, photo site, etc.). If you just need a website for blogging so that you can update it yourself on a regular basis, selecting a WordPress-powered site will be most cost-effective. I have worked with clients that already have a business website and have needed a separate Blog site implemented. Others have had me create a WordPress-powered website with an embedded Blog that they can control. In both cases, I've trained my clients on the use of the tool and they have found it very user-friendly. Because WordPress software (and other systems like it) are free to use the cost of building powerful websites is much less than conventional methods of programming, and they are also much quicker to implement.

CHOOSE THE RIGHT PLATFORM

As stated in the answers above, build your new website using a content management system (CMS) as the backbone. There are many good CMS tools available. Besides the most popular tools mentioned, namely WordPress and Joomla, there are others you can also check out: MoveableType, Drupal and Mambo. Don't you love these creative names? More interesting names like these will blossom as new applications are introduced!

WordPress

WordPress *(http://www.wordpress.org)* is the largest self-hosted blogging tool worldwide and it is widely used by a whole range of businesses, from entrepreneurs and small businesses to Fortune 500 companies.[1] While WordPress first started as a blogging system to enhance the typography of everyday writing, it is now a full content management system making it the platform on which many companies are choosing to build their websites. With lots of Plug-ins, Widgets, and Themes (explained in Chapter Six), WordPress helps extend the functionality of your site while enhancing the user experience. WordPress is a very user-friendly tool used to build powerful, functional websites and blogs, ranging from basic personal sites to complex online applications. Each updated version is enriched with new functionality. There are hundreds of free templates available for WordPress. Google "free wordpress themes" and you'll have lots of choices.

A WordPress-based website or blog gives you full control of your content so you can post on a regular basis. "Regular basis" is relevant to your particular situation or business. You may want to write new blog posts daily, once per week, or once per month. It really much depends on your type of business. For instance, an online magazine is most likely to have fresh content on a daily basis. Whatever you decide is right for your audience, be consistent with it. More in-depth details about WordPress will be covered in Chapter Six.

Joomla

Joomla *(http://www.joomla.org)* is another very popular CMS tool used to build great websites and other complex online applications.[2] Tools like WordPress and Joomla are known as "open source systems." This means they are freely available for anyone to use. The only time you pay is when you hire a consultant or developer to customize your website.

Joomla is the backbone for many sophisticated websites including for well-known companies such as Citibank, Harvard University and IHOP, the restaurant chain. Joomla has been used worldwide to create a variety of websites including corporate websites and intranets, e-commerce, online reservations systems, online magazines and newspapers, government applications, small business websites, non-profit organizations, schools, churches, personal and family pages.

KEYWORDS AND YOUR WEBSITE

Now that you know why keywords are important, here are some tips for creating search engine-friendly sites:

1. **Make your website keyword-rich and have ample content.**

   Simply put, this attracts visitors. Webmasters of other high-traffic sites also like to link to content-rich sites. Your website ranking will improve when other websites link to yours.

2. **Determine the keywords your audience uses to search.**

   Select the keywords that fit your business and speak to your audience. Write your content around these keyword phrases.

3. **Make your site easily accessible to users.**

   Build a logical link structure.

4. **Avoid filling your page with lists of keywords.**

   Google considers this a deceptive practice. Sprinkle your keyword phrases throughout the content in a natural manner.

5. **Don't purchase search engine optimization services from companies that "guarantee" high rankings for your site.**

Even Google itself does not guarantee high rankings. There are over 200 factors Google uses to determine page rankings. Of course, only Google knows what they are. If Google discovers your domain name to be affiliated with the type of services that exercise deceptive practices, your domain could be banned from Google's index. Only work with legitimate SEO consulting firms that can help improve your site's *flow* and *content* to help increase your search rankings. This is the key to increase your organic search results by implementing on-page and off-page optimization practices.

6. **Follow Google's guidelines for images.**

Name your images with appropriate keywords.

7. **Don't create multiple copies of a page under different URLs.**

Block duplicate pages by using a robots.txt file. This will ensure that your preferred page is included in Google's search results. Your website designer should be able to assist you with this.

8. **Index your site.**

For Google to index and rank your site, it is important to ensure that Google can "crawl" your site. You can add the URL index code to your website by following Google's instructions at *http://www.google.com/addurl*. Google does not guarantee that your URL will be added to their index, but don't give up. Also, keep in mind that things such as broken or dead links in your site may impact your ranks negatively.

GUIDELINES TO BUILD AN EFFECTIVE WEBSITE

1. **Give your visitors a reason to come back.**

   Know what your customers want, think like them and speak their language in your text. This is fundamental for creating successful sales copy that entices your readers to return for more. Luckily, you can discover what your customers want by using keyword search tools (discussed in Chapter Three).

2. **Allow visitors to register for your newsfeeds or newsletter.**

   Visitors who like your content will want to stay connected with you. Offer a free monthly newsletter with tips for your market niche.

3. **Lead customers to take action.**

   You need to decide what it is you want your visitors to do, and make this the focal point on your home page. Many websites are so crowded with information on the home page (this does not necessarily apply to news websites) that visitors see "nothing" because of all the graphics, videos and other components that scream for attention. This can confuse visitors who may not be clear on what to do *first*. The secret to a good website is for it to be *clean* (not crowded) and *clear* (provide direction) from the moment they land on your home page. Guide visitors to the ultimate goal: to contact you or make a purchase. Make your "Contact Us" page easy to find. Place your social networking buttons in a prominent location to encourage a response to your "Join us on Facebook" or "Follow us on Twitter" call to actions. Make your "take action" or "next step" clear.

4. **Keep it clean.**

   Concentrate on making your visitors' experience easy and

painless. Keep it simple and easy to navigate.

5. Skip intros.

People want information fast and they will almost always skip the introductions. Consider allocating these moneys to creating quality graphics and videos instead.

6. Have a focal point.

Websites that are designed with visitors in mind have a focal point on the home page. You can easily tell when websites miss this critical step. Their home pages are crowded with every piece of graphic clamoring for attention. Think simple, easy and classy, and remember that less is usually better.

7. Add videos.

Research shows that if you have videos on your site, people may linger longer.

8. Add links to your social networking pages.

Make it easy for visitors to link to your social networking pages by making your social buttons easy to spot. Consider displaying your Facebook fans or latest tweets on the left or right sidebars of your website.

9. Make it easy for visitors to contact you.

Your website needs to have a way for customers to get answers to their questions quickly and easily. An effective way to do this is to have a "frequently asked questions" page. Another strategy is to have a contact form on your site where they can submit questions or simply contact you online. This serves as a great tool to gather information from your visitors.

10. Include a site map.

A site map makes it easier for visitors to narrow their focus. Include the menu option links that normally appear on the header section in the footer as well.

11. Refine, test, refine, test...

Websites are a work in progress. They are not perfect or complete from the beginning. Building a website with good content and historical data, and creating regular readership takes time, effort and dedication. In the process of navigating through the online jungle, you will find additional ideas that might work for your business. Don't be afraid to incorporate these new ideas and test them out on your website. If a particular idea did not work, try a new one until you discover something that works for you and the audience you serve.

WHAT TO LOOK FOR WHEN CHOOSING A WEB DESIGNER

1. Hire an agency or a consultant who knows SEO.

Optimization is critical to rank well in organic search results. Remember, it is a combination of various activities that help to improve your results.

2. Get it in writing.

Your proposals and contracts should be clear with details to include: what pages will be built, how many graphics will be included, how your social media accounts will be embedded and be linkable from your site, what content will be included and who is responsible for providing or creating it. These details provide a roadmap and sets expectations for all parties. It can even help to note important aspects in design or processes that may have been overlooked.

3. **Don't pay the entire fee up front.**

    Professional web designers typically require a deposit with a payout plan during project milestones. A web designer who asks for the entire fee up front is a red flag.

4. **Obtain references.**

    What others say will give you confidence in your web designer choice.

5. **Look at previous or work in progress.**

    Seeing the work of previous projects should provide you a glimpse into the web designer's style and quality of work.

6. **Follow your gut feelings.**

    Sometimes you just have to follow your "gut" feelings. Successful entrepreneurs share that during times when everyone else thought it was the wrong decision but their "gut" told them it was the right choice, it turns out it was.

Steps to Enhance Your Website

Your next step is to establish your presence in the social media landscape, and link to those external sources from your existing website and vice versa. This includes creating a complementary blog, which you can build with the same look and feel of your existing website, and establishing or enhancing your presence in the most popular social networks (i.e., Facebook, Twitter, and LinkedIn).

Here's how to start:

1. Log on to your website and make an honest assessment of the overall user-friendliness and content as it relates to the information shared in this chapter.

2. List the things that you are doing right and those that need attention.

3. Create an action plan to enhance your online branding including your website and social networking platforms.

4. Hire competent help to assist with your goals and provide training in areas outside your expertise.

5 – BLOGGING BASICS

"New marketing is about the relationships, not the medium."
Ben Grossman, Founder of BiGMarK

Business blogging needs to be an integral part of your marketing strategy. Here's why: Three in four women online actively use blogs, message boards, and social networks *daily*.[1] People trust the opinions of personal acquaintances and consumers posted online (including blogs) more than they do advertising.[2] According to eMarketer "43% of U.S. companies will be blogging by 2012."[3] eMarketer.com's research found that 51% of U.S. internet users (113 million people) were actively reading blogs on a monthly basis in 2010. Their research estimates that by 2014, the percentage of blog readers will increase to 60%, that's a whopping 150 million people.[4] Smart businesses realize that people are reading blogs and are actively sharing their findings with their family and friends.

Although it is vital to build your network on sites such as Facebook, Twitter, and LinkedIn, you also need a blog that you can control and sets you and your company apart. Your blog will help to establish yourself as an expert, grow your network of loyal followers, generate quality leads, sell your products and services, and improve your search rankings. Search engines love and seek new content continuously, and so do other webmasters. This is very important to encourage external sites to link back to yours. In addition, people who are interested in your product or service will pay attention to the useful tips and expertise you offer through your postings.

Blogs enable you to nurture a more personal connection with your market niche. You can build rapport and trust with your audience by becoming their viable resource. And when they decide to make a purchase or a recommendation, you'll be their first choice. Remember that people enjoy doing business with those they like and trust, and blogs lend themselves for interaction and for personalizing your business.

SUCCESSFUL BLOGGING

The secret to successful blogging is creating compelling content that is magnetic and encourages engagement. Keep in mind these fundamental principles to ensure your success:

First, be *authentic* with the information you share and ensure it *adds value* to your target audience (compelling content).

Second, share information with *purpose and intention*. Take the opportunity to educate your customers on practical solutions to solve *their* problems. People are interested in making their lives easier, better and more effective. Draft your web copy in a manner that provides answers and encourages your visitors to take action—to call you or buy your product or service. Your solutions, together with excellence in service, are the elements that help brand you and your company in the minds of your customers. This is what leads to customer loyalty and continued business.

Third, have a clear *call to action*. You can share excellent information in your content and miss the opportunity to engage your audience. The way to increase feedback is simply by asking. End every one of your blog posts with a question to encourage a response.

Include other calls to action throughout your site. Debbie Weil provides the following ideas on persuasive calls to action such as: "Join us on Facebook (Twitter, YouTube, etc.);" "Sign up for our e-newsletter;" "Ask us a question."[5]

WHAT TO BLOG ABOUT

Blog on topics that you are passionate about, showcase your expertise, and are *relevant* to the audience you serve. Be creative in your approach. Tell your story and views in your own voice and style while also speaking the language of your audience by including the keyword phrases they used to search to get to your page.

Share stories or news pertinent to the interests of your market niche. Include stories and testimonials from your clients. Attend local events and interview experts in your industry. If you can video record the interviews, even better. Create a YouTube channel and upload your video interviews to it, but also include them in your blog posts. Don't worry about your videos not being perfect. People want to connect with the real you.

You can use Google Alerts to stay abreast of your industry and topics that you and your audience are interested in. Google Alerts is an excellent tool that will alert you via email each time it finds the terms you have set it to monitor. You can set your search words to include your name, company name, keyword phrases relevant to your market niche and even your competitors' names. Staying aware and commenting on the discussions relative to your area of expertise will enable you to immediately connect with potential followers for your blog and quickly build your rapport as an expert on a particular subject. Access the Google Alerts tool at *http://www.google.com/alerts.*

BLOGGING PLATFORMS

Blogging tools are free software licensed under the General Public License, *(http://www.gnu.org)*. Consider using WordPress *(http://wordpress.org)* or even Google's Blogger *(http://blogger.com)*. Chapter Six delves deeper on WordPress. WordPress is an Open Source system, this means that there are many individuals around the globe working on it and you pay no fees for the use of the software. An Open Source system licensed under the General Public License *(www.gnu.org)* gives its users the ability to access the software code, enhance it and release the improvements to its community of users.

BLOGGING TIPS

- **Make your postings reader-friendly.**

  Internet readers are "scanners". They want information fast and scroll down on pages to find the piece of information they're looking for or find interesting. Draft your blog posts into short, easy-to-read paragraphs. Incorporate headings, bullets or paragraph numbering that makes the content easy to scan. See Figures 5.1 and 5.2. For examples of reader-friendly blog posts visit my website at *http://www.socialexecs.com/blog*.

- **Create keyword-rich compelling headlines, sub-headlines and first sentences.**

  Because internet users "scan" pages, the headlines, sub-headlines and the first sentence within each paragraph becomes very important, especially in lengthy blog posts.

  Use your top-producing keywords in your headlines and sprinkle them throughout the content. (Refer to Chapter Three, "Optimization and Keywords").

Make your headlines interesting and concise. Consider using titles such as "Top 5…", "3 Ways to…", "6 Tips for…", "How to …", "Must-have…", and the like.

- **Use a word processor to write and spell-check your work.**

Write your blog posts in a word processor such as Microsoft Office Word to spell-check your content. WordPress indicates misspelled words with a red underline (see Figure 5.3). However, in WordPress you don't have the flexibility to run a full spell-check on the post you're writing as you do in Microsoft Word.

- **Use Windows Notepad to import your content.**

Once you have spell-checked your blog post, copy and paste it in Notepad, and from Notepad copy and paste it into your blog. When you copy/paste directly from Microsoft Word, sometimes it puts underlying code in the article that can mess up your page.

Figure 5.1 Example of a reader-friendly blog Post

Figure 5.2 Example of a reader-friendly blog Post

Figure 5.3 Misspelled word indicated with a red underline inside WordPress' Edit Post option

- **Be honest, truthful and authentic.**

  People are not interested in self-centered talk but do want your honesty. Surf other blogs to get an idea on how others are drafting their content.

- **Develop your own voice and writing style.**

  Have a one-on-one conversation with your readers. Be yourself. Don't shy away from sharing whatever springs to your mind. However, remember your business purpose for your blog.

- **Write as often as you'd like.**

  Create an editorial calendar and schedule writing days just as you do your doctor's appointment. Prepare a list of topics you'd like to blog about in advance and schedule them in your writing days.

- **Use everyday language.**

  Use language that is easy for your readers to understand. Keep it simple.

- **Use common sense.**

  Remember that your blog posts are open to the world. Don't write anything that you wouldn't want your customers, business associates and partners, spouse or close friends to know.

- **Allow comments.**

  Let your readers share their opinion. But be prepared for positive and negative feedback. As administrator of your blog, you can set filters for you to approve comments prior to them becoming visible on your site. At this point you can delete any comments that are either spam, trash your competitors, or don't meet your comment guidelines. However, remember that greater lessons are learned from the unhappy customer than from the happy one.

- **Establish comment guidelines.**

In order to maintain the integrity of your Blog it would be helpful for you to provide direction to your visitors on your comment guidelines. You may not want profanity on your site. Letting your community know will help avoid unpleasant situations. Here are a few examples of comment guidelines for your social media community: NoFactZone.net, a Stephen Colbert fan site, *http://www.nofactzone.net/about/no-fact-zone-comment-policy*; Texas Green Source, *http://www.texasgreensource.com/about/comment-guidelines*; Cisco Networking Academy Facebook Fan Page: *http://www.facebook.com/cisconetworkingacademy* (welcome tab).

- **Outsource graphical needs.**

Hire the experts to customize your blog or website. This is very important to maintain a professional image.

- **Add photos and videos.**

Photos and videos make your blog posts more interesting. Use them for illustration and to help your visitors feel more connected with you. Ree Drummond, owner of ThePioneerWoman.com makes excellent use of photos, *http://thepioneerwoman.com*.

- **Request and Acknowledge feedback.**

Don't get wrapped up in sharing and fail to ask for feedback. End every one of your blog posts with a question to encourage feedback. Thank those who take the time to provide comments.

BUILD TRUST WITH YOUR AUDIENCE

- **Listen to your audience.**

One way to show that you're listening is through

acknowledgment—by responding to people's comments. This could be a thank you note to comments posted, or even a question to continue the conversation.

- **Speak as an individual.**

This will give your visitors a direct, human connection with your business, rather than a "faceless" image. Focus on building strong relationships that can result in increased customer loyalty.

- **Make your website as professional looking as you can.**

This will send the message that you are serious about your business.

- **Make your contributions informative and helpful.**

Don't hard-sell. Don't push your products or services, and don't trash your competitors either. Build rapport first. When sharing information about your products or services focus on how these solve their problems and improve their lives.

BLOG & BLOGGING FAQ'S

1. **What is the difference between a blog and a website? Do I need to have two separate sites?**

There are different types of websites such as e-commerce, corporate, non-profit, personal, etc.

A blog, short for "web log", is a website with web 2.0 capabilities, meaning that it allows interaction with your audience. Web 1.0 websites lack this engagement component. Blog sites normally display post entries on the home page in descending chronological order, where the most recent entries come first.

In addition, with blogging tools, such as WordPress, you can create a full-blown corporate website by customizing the home page and menu options, while embedding the company blog within the same site. The home page and menu options can look like any other website and make your blog posts appear in a "Blog" menu option. Refer to my website to see how this works at *http://www.socialexecs.com/blog.*

You'll notice that the home page looks like any other website. The "Blog" page hosts my blog posts and displays them in descending chronological order. With this site design option I only need to maintain *one* website—a great time saver!

Another alternative is to have your main corporate website and your blog site separately. This preference is good especially if you already have an established company website, or if you want to make a clear distinction between the two. When doing this, be sure to have your blog site mirror the look and feel of your corporate website for branding purposes.

A good example is Whole Foods Market corporate website and its Blog website that is setup as a sub-domain:

Corporate website: *http://www.wholefoodsmarket.com,*

Blog website: *http://blog.wholefoodsmarket.com.*

2. **Which hosting services support WordPress installation?**

    There are several hosting services that support automatic installation of CMS tools such as WordPress. This means that with a few clicks, the WordPress software and the database where your data is stored are created and installed automatically in your hosting server. This eliminates manual steps to your WordPress software installation.

    Some of the hosting services that offer automatic installation include: Bluehost, Hostgator, DreamHost, MediaTemple, and Laughing Squid. For the most up-to-date list of service providers that support automatic installation of software like WordPress, check out *http://wordpress.org/hosting*.

3. When should I blog?

This really depends on the level of engagement you want with your audience. The more, the better. Create an editorial calendar. Schedule writing time just as you do your doctor's appointment. Create a list of topics in advanced, organized in different categories that you want to blog about. Write posts that are related to the products and solutions you offer.

4. Where do I find information to blog about?

You can blog about whatever comes to mind. However, blog about things that will be of benefit and interest to your audience. Also, don't lock yourself to just blog about business. Be creative and versatile. You can find plenty of information to talk about from your local community events, industry trends, websites, Twitter connections, etc. Another good source is the Google Alerts function that alerts you via email based on the search terms you choose.

5. I'm not really a writer. How can I blog?

A cost-effective way to do this is to write your blog posts and then hire someone to edit your work and "SEO" your blog posts. SEO bloggers know the guidelines to follow when drafting content that is user- and search engine-friendly. Your other option is to outsource it. You can take some of your marketing dollars to hire writers that specialize in content writing. These experts benefit you because they know what they're doing and can run with the information you provide to manage your social media marketing program. There are plenty of freelancers available that exercise their writing muscles on a daily basis. Maximize your strengths and outsource the tasks that require specialized expertise.

Let's Get Practical

Business Blogging Do's

- Write using your own voice.

- Feel free to share tips and ideas with your audience. Make your postings interesting with content that adds value to your readers.

- Embed the language of your visitors—the keywords they used to search and get to your web page. Be concise and to the point.

- Keep your commitment to blog on a regular basis; whatever you decide "regular" is to you.

- Maintain your professionalism, even when you have to reply to negative comments.

- Reply to all comments posted on your blogs and social networking sites.

- Use your people skills when communicating with your audience.

- Plan a blogging schedule.

Business Blogging Don'ts

- Don't sell. Be resourceful and informative. Focus on establishing yourself as an expert.

- Don't copy and paste text from other sources. Be authentic. Give credit to your resources of information and include links to direct pages.

- Don't feel like you have to blog about business only. Be creative.

People like to do business with humans that are "for real."

Examples of Successful Blogs

The following blogs are a few of my favorites that exemplify the principles of successful blogging shared in this chapter. This variety of blogs is sure to inspire and give you ideas to make yours unique.

The Pioneer Woman. Ree Drummond candidly talks about her ranch life, family, homeschooling, cooking, and much more with hundreds of interesting photos. *http://www.thepioneerwoman.com*

Freebies 4 Moms. A blog created by Heather Hernandez for anyone who wants to save money with freebies. *http://freebies4mom.com*

One Man's Blog. John Podzadzides' blog (aka John P. for short) who shares just about anything! *http://www.onemansblog.com*

Copyblogger. An excellent resource for online bloggers where Brian Clark (an attorney) shares all sorts of tips and advice written both by himself and his guest bloggers. *http://www.copyblogger.com*

Social Media Examiner. An excellent resource that shares what's happening in social media. *http://www.socialmediaexaminer.com*

No Fact Zone. The #1 fan site for Stephen Colbert and The Colbert Report. *http://www.nofactzone.net.*

Whole Foods Blog. The official Whole Foods Market blog filled with tips for healthy living. *http://blog.wholefoodsmarket.com.*

Man of the House. By Proctor & Gamble, a blog created to add value to its audience: men. The blog provides a plethora of articles to help modern men enhance their lives. *http://manofthehouse.com.*

6 – MANAGING YOUR CONTENT

"Monitor, engage, and be transparent; these have always been the keys to success in the digital space."

Dallas Lawrence, Levick Strategic Communications

While there are several good Content Management Systems (CMS) to choose from, I will use WordPress as the example in this chapter. In Chapter Five, we covered the basics of blogging. We will now focus on how to manage your content using WordPress. In the back of the book I provide instructions on how to obtain your free *Mastering WordPress Toolkit*, a guide with step-by-step instructions on setting up the free version of WordPress for you to start blogging right away.

WordPress has evolved as a full content management system through the development and availability of many Themes, Widgets and Plugins, which are small programs that help extend the functionality and professional presentation of your website.

If you already have an established website and you want to create a blog to attract more traffic, consider using WordPress. Have your blog site mirror the look and feel of your current website, and have them both reference each other.

To create a brand new site, also consider using WordPress because it is easy to learn and allows even the most non-technical person to manage and update their content with ease. WordPress-powered sites look like any other professionally created website. The great advantage is that content can be updated regularly via the administration tool. Content includes information, video and images.

Figure 6.1 shows a sample of a WordPress-powered site. Figure 6.2 provides the administrative view of a WordPress website—the "Dashboard."

WORDPRESS LINGO

Following are some of the basic terms to know about WordPress.

Theme

A Theme is the graphical interface, the skin, of your website. You can swap themes but your data remains the same.

Widget

A Widget is a small program that you can easily install to add new functionality and enhance visitor experience. A good example of a widget is the Google advertisements that you may have seen in other websites. These ads are viewable by users when a small piece of code is included on a page or a widget section of your site. A widget can be anything from a blog roll, calendar, voting poll, latest blog posts, site map, images, etc.

Plugin

A Plugin is a group of PHP functions (code) that extends the functionality of your website. Plugins are similar to widgets. Figures 6.3 and 6.4 display Plugin examples.

Figure 6.1 WordPress-powered website with embedded blog

Figure 6.2 WordPress' Dashboard, the administrator control center

Figure 6.3 Social bookmarking Plugin by ShareThis.com

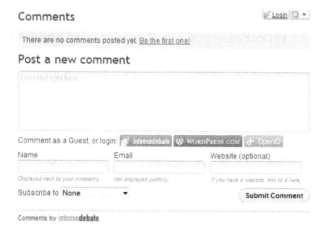

Figure 6.4 Comments Plugin by IntenseDebate.com

THEMES AND CUSTOM DESIGN

There are hundreds of theme templates from which to choose. You'll find a lot of them available at zero cost. The disadvantage of free themes is they come with advertising information that you may not be able to get rid of and there may be other limitations.

A purchased theme offers greater flexibility and the ability to tweak the code. Once you add your own logo, change colors, and add custom graphics, you'll have a very nice low-cost website up and running quickly. I encourage you to find a theme template that meets your needs and have it customized as necessary. Explore this option even if you are thinking that you prefer to have a more custom design made. A knowledgeable WordPress developer should be able to customize a theme to your needs.

POSTS AND PAGES

In WordPress, you write Posts and Pages.

A Post is a *blog entry*.

A Page is *static* content such as "About" and "Services" pages where contents remain constant, but can still be edited and updated.

Therefore, Pages are not Posts, and Pages and Posts are not files. Their contents are stored in your WordPress database. You can edit both Posts and Pages even after saving and publishing them. Although Pages and Posts are very similar in that they have Titles, Content and maintain a cohesive look throughout, they do differ. Posts will appear in the "Blog" page in descending chronological order. Pages are accessed via the menu bar, for most themes. Figures 6.5 through 6.7 provide Post and Page examples.

Understanding Posts

- Posts appear in reverse chronological order on the blog's home page by default. However, you can set a different page for your Blog posts so as to display something else on your home page, thereby making your theme more customized.

- Posts usually have comments fields beneath them, whereas Pages do not. There are, however, some Plugins that you can install that allow comments on pages as well.

- Posts are associated with Categories and Tags, Pages are not. See Figures 6.8 through 6.10.

Figure 6.5 User view of a blog post in a WordPress-powered site

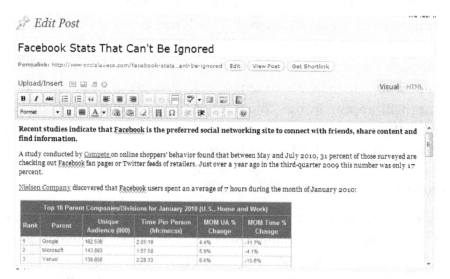

Figure 6.6 Administrator view of a blog post in the Dashboard

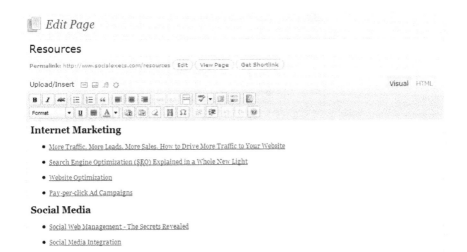

Figure 6.7 Administrator view of a page in the Dashboard

Figure 6.8 Posts are associated to Categories

Figure 6.9 Posts are associated to Tags

Figure 6.10 Pages are *not* associated to Categories or Tags

Understanding Pages

- Pages reside outside the blog chronology, that is, they do not cycle through your Posts.

- Pages can be set to appear on the main menu bar. Examples of these pages include About, Services, Contact Us, Photo Gallery, and the like.

- Pages can be organized into Sub-Pages that show as pull-down options underneath each applicable main menu option on the menu bar. See Figure 6.11 where it shows the "Services" page to have a sub-page "Social Media Webinars."

- You can set other common pages in the footer section of your website such as Privacy, Legal and Disclaimer pages.

- Pages are not associated with Categories and Tags as Posts are.

CHANGING THE HOME AND BLOG PAGES

In WordPress, you have the flexibility to change your home and blog pages. The home page will show whatever page you select. The Blog page will display your posts or entries in reverse chronological order. To do this, you first have to create a new page, name it (i.e., Blog), leave its content blank, select "Blog" from the Template menu options in the Page Attributes box (to the right), and publish it. Figure 6.12 shows this.

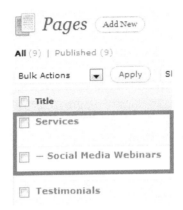

Figure 6.11 Pages can have sub-Pages

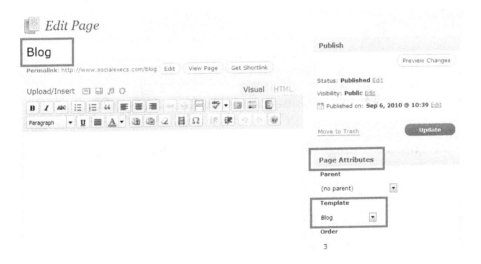

Figure 6.12 How to create your "Blog" page

After creating and publishing the Blog page, the next step is to establish your home page and your Blog page in the "Reading

Settings". Figure 6.13 displays these options.

Figure 6.13 Setting your home and Posts pages

You can use whatever label you want for your posts page such as "Blog," "Articles," "News." Figure 6.14 provides an example on how your posts page will display on the menu bar of your WordPress website.

Figure 6.14 "Blog" menu option that will display post entries

USER ROLES AND CAPABILITIES

You can set users with different levels of access. In WordPress, there are five different levels of roles with varying capabilities:

- **Administrator**. Has access to all the administrative features.

- **Editor**. Can publish and manage their posts and pages, and those of other users.

- **Author**. Can publish and manage their posts.

- **Contributor**. Can write and manage their posts, but cannot publish them.

- **Subscriber**. Can only manage their profile.

FREE HOSTING VS SELF-HOSTED BLOG SERVICE

Free Hosting

WordPress offers a free hosting blog service. Although a free blog is not necessarily the choice for a permanent professional business image on the internet (especially if you intend to dedicate time and effort into blogging), it does provide you with the opportunity to get your feet wet and learn the tool.

Advantages of a Free Hosting Account

- You can create a free blog quickly.
- You spend no money out of pocket.
- You can familiarize yourself on how blogging platforms work.
- You can experience the advantages of a content management system.
- You can upgrade to a self-hosted service.

Limitations of a Free Hosting Account

- You will not have a top-level domain such as *www.yourname.com*. Your domain name will include wordpress.com: *www.yourname.wordpress.com*.

- There are less configuration choices where you are limited as to what you can change on your blog. This may not seem like a big deal when you first begin. However, as your blogging capabilities and demand grows, these limitations will hinder flexibility.

- The Plugins option is not available with the Free Hosting Account. Plugins extend the functionality of your website.

- You will have to choose your theme from a selection of canned themes, which does not allow your website to be unique and will end up looking like other blogs.
- You don't have complete ownership of your blog. Although you do have ownership of your content, WordPress owns the domain name associated with your blog, not you.
- You don't have complete control of your blog and are limited as to what you can do.

Figure 6.15 shows the functional differences between a free WordPress account and a self-hosted one.

Self-Hosted

A self-hosted website is the most professional and serious way to have a blog.

Advantages of a Self-Hosted Account

- You have your own registered domain name like any other serious business, such as *www.yourname.com*.
- You can add more custom-looking Themes.
- You can add Plugins for additional functionality of your website.
- You own your blog and its content.
- You maintain control of your blog and can do whatever you want with it.

Figure 6.15 Free hosted vs. a self-hosted WordPress account

At this point you may be asking yourself some very valid questions with respect to having a personal blog.

1. **Should I use my personal domain name to host my WordPress blog? If yes, can the blog be my personal website?**

   Yes. There are two kinds of WordPress sites: the free service, which will be *www.yourname.wordpress.com* and the self-hosted service, *www.yourname.com* without the word "wordpress" in it. The second option is for serious professionals and businesses. If you have a domain name reserved in your personal name, by all means use it for your blog.

2. **With all the social media sites available for free, do I even need a personal website or blog?**

   A few thoughts for you to ponder:

   - Your blog, *www.yourname.com*, is for your personal branding as a professional. In this blog, you are free to share whatever you want, both professionally and personally, establish it as basis of information for your fans and followers, and build rapport. Twitter and Facebook are to share information of what's happening in the moment. People will not look back to your Twitter feeds or your Facebook posts to see what you said two weeks ago. This is why it is important to set your website or blog as the permanent source of information for your audience.

   - From your personal blog, people can get to the other resources you provide—your business websites.

   - You have full control of your own site.

   - Your blog is searchable for archived articles on your site, and also in search engines.

7 – TOOLS OF THE TRADE

"Social media is like a snowball rolling down the hill. It's picking up speed. Five years from now, it's going to be the standard."
Jeff Antaya, Chief Marketing Officer of Plante Moran

Social media tools are not scarce. The question is which tools should you use that prove to drive the most traffic? How do you take the next step to attract the valuable traffic to *your* website?

In this chapter, I will present the core group of social media tools and technologies for you to consider and make a part of your online marketing program.

Your social media strategy is not about isolated activities in your social networking involvement. Rather, it is comprised of an *inter-related* approach that enhances your overall branding and strengthens your relationship with your customers and prospects. This is the purpose of participating in social media marketing. As you establish yourself as a viable resource to your fans and followers, your information should encourage them to visit your website. Once your visitors arrive on your website, the systems you have in place should persuade them to contact you or make a purchase.

The synergy created by the inter-connectivity of various technologies working for you, together with good content and Google-friendly website practices, are the things that will help increase your website traffic.

Later in this chapter, I will show you how to automate some of your management tasks, and in Chapter Eleven, I'll offer some tips for handling your social media strategy.

CORE SET OF SOCIAL MEDIA TOOLS

There is a core group of tools that should be at the heart of your online marketing program. You can always add new technologies that become available to your marketing mix later, as you need them.

Figure 7.1 Social Media Core Tools

The social media technologies shown in Figure 7.1 represent the core tools that should be part of your social media toolbox. This is not to suggest that you must use every one of these. Some of the tools accomplish similar goals. The variety available gives you the freedom to use the technologies that you feel most comfortable with and that make the most sense for your business use. An example is YouTube and Vimeo. They both accomplish the same goal, but you can choose the one you like best, that resonates more with your needs, or simply you find easier to use. Another example is Flickr and Picasa. They're both great tools. Feel free to use both or just choose one. Some of the tools to manage your social media presence such as TweetDeck, HootSuite and Nutshell Mail all help you manage your accounts, but they are each unique with diverse functionalities.

You may prefer using one technology over another, or you may find it beneficial to use a combination. For example, if you prefer to receive updates a few times per day, then you'd probably like Nutshell Mail, which you can set to notify you whenever and however many times you wish. However, if you like to know what's happening in your social network in real-time, then TweetDeck is a great option.

You may find that using a combination of tools, such as TweetDeck *and* HootSuite, is the best answer for easing your management activities. TweetDeck can enable you to know what's happening in real time, while HootSuite will allow you to schedule tweets for the future as pending tweets. Check out this article for an in-depth comparison between TweetDeck and HootSuite: *http://www.dragonblogger.com/comparing-hootsuite-to-tweetdeck*.

Part of your planning includes deciding which tools will align with your business goals. You will find that a large percentage of the core group of recommended technologies shown in Figure 7.1 will be essential and beneficial to reach your target audience, and meet your business needs.

MAIN ACTIVITIES IN THE SOCIAL MEDIA LANDSCAPE

To execute an effective, integrated strategy, your social media activities include:

- Publishing
- Social networking
- Micro-blogging
- Social bookmarking
- Video sharing
- Photo sharing
- Automation
- Managing your accounts
- Measuring your efforts

Take a look at each of these activities and the recommended tools for each one in more detail.

PUBLISHING

Publishing content is one of the most important activities of your social media marketing approach. In Chapter Six, I discussed the types of content to publish on your website or blog, and the importance of using Content Management Systems (CMS) such as WordPress. Also, I mentioned how painless it is to manage your content using WordPress, which allows you to easily add new pages, blog posts and photos, and link to other external sources.

I want to also mention **SlideShare** as a useful free tool that can be used in your publishing activity. It allows you to share your Power

Point presentations. This is especially beneficial for consultants, speakers and trainers. But don't limit yourself if you don't fall into these categories. Any business can share presentations about their product or service. Create your account and start uploading some of the presentations you may have in your business toolbox at *http://www.slideshare.com*. See Figures 7.2 and 7.3.

Figure 7.2 Uploaded Presentations on SlideShare.com

SOCIAL NETWORKING & MICRO-BLOGGING

Facebook and Twitter are the two dominating platforms in online social networking. A study performed by John Podzadzides, co-creator of Woopra, a real-time website traffic analytics tool, and author of the popular OneMansBlog.com, shows some astounding details. Podzadzides' analysis of over 100,000 websites using Woopra found that 68% of the traffic referred to external websites came from Facebook, while 25% originated from Twitter (see Figure 7.4).

Figure 7.3 Presentation View on SlideShare.com

We have previously discussed the social networking sites you should be publishing content to, such as Facebook, Twitter and LinkedIn, and over the next three chapters, we will discuss each of these individually in detail.

SOCIAL BOOKMARKING

Social bookmarking is a method for Internet users to organize, store, manage and search for bookmarks of resources online (Wikipedia). Unlike file sharing, the *resources* themselves aren't shared they are merely bookmarks *referencing* them. There are over 200 bookmarking sites.

Podzadsides' study of where website traffic is generated also found that the top social bookmark referrers are StumbleUpon and Digg (see Figure 7.5).

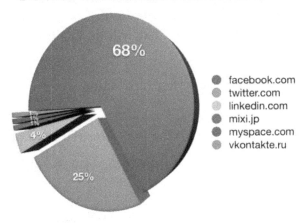

Figure 7.4 Social Network Referrers

Source courtesy of www.ReadWriteWeb.com[1]

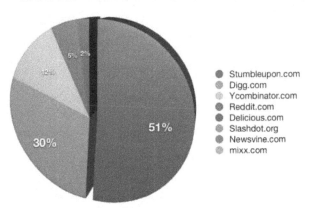

Figure 7.5 Social Bookmark Referrers

Source courtesy of www.ReadWriteWeb.com[1]

Knowing this, it is vital to enable your visitors to share your posts and/or pages using these social bookmarking tools. In WordPress you can make it easy for your visitors to share your blog posts by installing the Plugin "AddThis" that will do just that. Learn more at *http://addthis.com.*

Other popular WordPress sharing Plugins are:

- **Sexy Bookmarks**. Enables visitors to share your content in various social bookmarking platforms (Figure 7.6).

- **TweetMeme Retweet Button**. Lets visitors retweet your blog posts (Figure 7.7)

- **fbLikeButton**. Allows you to configure and display the FaceBook Like Button before and/or after each post and/or page (Figure 7.7)

- **Smart YouTube**. Allows you to include video links from YouTube.

- **SI CAPTCHA Anti-Spam**. Adds security to your Blog by adding anti-spam methods, requiring users to have to type in a phrase shown on the image when commenting or registering on your site.

Figure 7.6 "Sexy Bookmarks" Plugin

Figure 7.7 fbLikeButton and TweetMeme Retweet Plugins

VIDEO SHARING

You Tube

YouTube is your video sharing site. It is the world's leading hub for sharing videos. According to Mashable.com, in March 2009 YouTube reached 100 million monthly viewers in the United States with 6.3 billion videos viewed.[2] (By the way, YouTube was acquired by Google in 2006[3] and a year earlier it had purchased 15 small companies spending $130.5 million in this effort![4]).

Podzadzides' study discovered that YouTube is the number one media referrer with a whopping 84% share (see Figure 7.8). Per Podzadzides, "YouTube drives *900% more traffic* to websites than Flickr."

Media Referrers

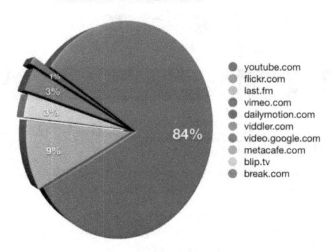

Figure 7.8 Media Referrers

Source courtesy of www.ReadWriteWeb.com[1]

In WordPress, there is a Plugin you can install to display YouTube uploaded videos on your WordPress website (or blog). The Plugin is called "Smart YouTube." **TIP:** upload your videos to your YouTube account first because it is a high-traffic site; then insert in the YouTube URL of your video in your website's page or blog post. That way, your video will have presence in YouTube and on your website, making it available to the world and your immediate network as well. Learn more and register for this free service at *http://www.youtube.com*.

Vimeo

Owned by InterActiveCorp, Vimeo is also a video social networking site. It allows commenting on each video page. Vimeo does not allow commercial videos, gaming videos, pornography, or anything not created by the user to be hosted on the site. Learn more and register for this free service at *http://www.vimeo.com*.

PHOTO SHARING

Flickr

Flickr is a photo storage and sharing site that currently hosts over 5 billion user photos. With its users uploading about 3,000 photos per minute, Flickr experienced its 5 billionth upload on September 18, 2010.[5]

Use Flickr to make a visual impression of your business to your audience. Tell your story in photo form. Here's a great example: *http://www.flickr.com/photos/garabedianproperties.*

Post photos of your products, events, community involvement and contributions, happy customers, open houses, consumer fairs, and the like. To set up your account log on to *http://www.flickr.com.* You'll first need to have your personal Yahoo free email account.

Picasa

Picasa is a free photo editing software owned by Google that now allows you to add name tags to your photos. This is also a great tool to share your photos with customers, business associates, family and friends. To learn more and sign up for Picasa Web Albums log on to *http://picasaweb.google.com.*

AUTOMATION

We all look for ways to save time and perform our tasks more efficiently. The good news is that there are many effective tools available to simplify your social media management.

FeedBurner

An RSS feed is a must-have component on your social media program to invite your users to connect with you. A popular source is

FeedBurner (*http://feedburner.google.com*). This automated program is a great time saver! RSS stands for Really Simple Syndication. RSS feeds publish frequently updated works in a standardized format. These works include blog posts, audio or video. Here's an example of one of my feeds *http://www.socialexecs.com/feed*.

Each time you post new content on your blog, everyone who has subscribed to your feed will receive the updates *automatically*. To see how this works subscribe to RSS feeds on your favorite sites.

Figure 7.9 provides an example of how to subscribe to an RSS Feed. Feel free to subscribe to my feed at *http://ww.socialexecs.com/blog* to see how it works. Type in your email and hit the "submit" button. Feedburner will send you a verification message after completing your subscription. Once you verify your email, you'll be subscribed to receive the latest postings.

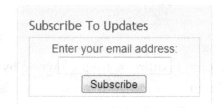

Figure 7.9 An opt-in RSS Feed Subscription form

Twitterfeed

While FeedBurner "burns" your RSS feed and notifies your subscribers automatically, Twitterfeed posts an entry on your social networking applications such as Twitter, Facebook's personal wall or your Facebook fan pages.

Twitterfeed's available services for the moment include Twitter, Statusnet, Ping.fm, Hellotxt and Facebook. At minimum, set up Twitterfeed to post to your Twitter and Facebook fan page accounts each time a new blog post is created on your site. Figures 7.10 through

7.13 illustrate how Twitterfeed works. Setup your free account at *http://twitterfeed.com.*

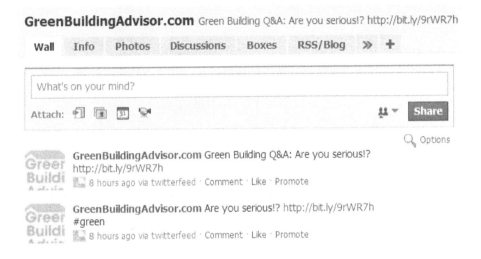

Figure 7.10 Automatic Twitterfeed entry on Facebook

Figure 7.11 Automatic Twitterfeed entry on Twitter

Figure 7.12 Latest RSS Feeds on Twitterfeed

Figure 7.13 RSS feed setup in Twitterfeed

MANAGING YOUR ACCOUNTS

It is a good idea to update your networking accounts at least once per week. Use automation tools to maximize your time. For example, HootSuite and Ping.fm send your postings to multiple social networking all at the same time. This is a huge time-saver.

Other great tools include TweetDeck, which lets you know what is happening in your network in real-time, and NutShell Mail, which notifies you via email with the latest postings on each of your major social networking sites such as Facebook, Twitter and LinkedIn. Set it up to notify you on the days and times you select.

HootSuite

Use HootSuite to update multiple social networks in one step including Twitter, Facebook, LinkedIn, WordPress, and Ping.fm. With HootSuite you can pre-schedule tweets and use the "shrink" functionality to shorten your URLs within the application. HootSuite enables you to manage multiple contributors. See Figures 7.14 and 7.15. Setup your free HootSuite account at *http://hootsuite.com*.

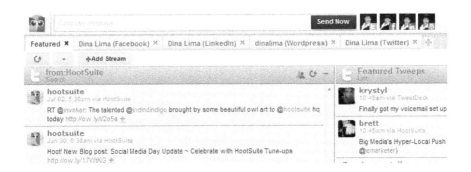

Figure 7.14 HootSuite's Dashboard

Figure 7.15 How to send a message from HootSuite

Ping.fm

Ping.fm is another great automation tool you can use to post messages to your multiple social networks. Ping.fm supports over 30 social networks (see Figures 7.16 and 7.17). Setup your free Ping account at *http://ping.fm*.

Google Buzz	Add Network	Delicious	Add Network
MySpace	Add Network	Koornk	Add Network
Ning	Add Network	YouAre	Add Network
GTalk Status	Add Network	Multiply	Add Network
AIM Status	Add Network	Yammer	Add Network
Tumblr	Add Network	StatusNet	Add Network
Identi.ca	Add Network	Vox	Add Network
Brightkite	Add Network	TypePad	Add Network
Plurk	Add Network	ShoutEm	Add Network
FriendFeed	Add Network	StreetMavens	Add Network
Jaiku	Add Network	myYearbook	Add Network
Blogger	Add Network	Posterous	Add Network
Plaxo Pulse	Add Network	Photobucket	Add Network
Bebo	Add Network	Yahoo Profiles	Add Network
hi5	Add Network	Tagged	Add Network
Xanga	Add Network	Yahoo Meme	Add Network
Custom URL	Add Network		

Figure 7.16 Ping.fm supports over 30 social networks

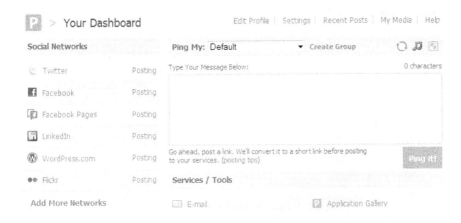

Figure 7.17 Ping.fm's Dashboard

TweetDeck

TweetDeck is your personal *real-time browser* for staying in touch with your contacts across Twitter, Facebook, LinkedIn, Google Buzz and Foursquare (see Figures 7.18 and 7.19). Unlike HootSuite, TweetDeck is a software application that needs to be downloaded and installed on your computer. HootSuite is an online application. You can use the TweetDeck Directory to find other professionals with whom to connect (Figure 7.20). To download your free TweetDeck application visit *http://www.tweetdeck.com*.

Nutshell Mail

Acquired by Constant Contact, Nutshell Mail eliminates the need to go into the separate social networking platforms to follow through on conversations and questions from your network. Setup your free Nutshell Mail account to receive your updates from Facebook, Twitter and LinkedIn all in *one* email at *http://nutshellmail.com*. You can reply to requests or follow up on comments from within your Nutshell Mail account. Refer to Figures 7.21 and 7.22.

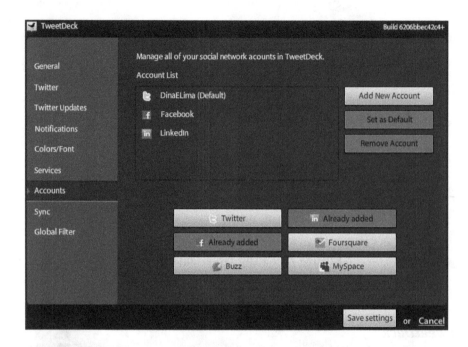

Figure 7.18 Social networking accounts to manage in TweetDeck

Figure 7.19 TweetDeck Desktop

TweetDeck **Directory**

Featured	ALL →	Arts & Entertainment	ALL →	Business & Professions	ALL →
World Cup	119	Music	4870	Advertising & Marketing	1456
Immigration Reform	104	Books & Writing	3370	Real Estate	1002
Israel-Palestine Crisis	66	Celebrities	2284	Education	864
Thai Protests	57	Video Games	1743	Markets & Economy	854
Afghanistan Escalation	39	Movies	1622	Law & Litigation	733
Gulf Oil Spill	39	Comedy	1464	Energy & Green Business	707

Cities	ALL →	Countries	ALL →	Food & Dining	ALL →
New York City	1038	Japan	1454	All Food & Dining	1605
Chicago	631	United States	1035	Wine	1059
Los Angeles	575	Brazil	813	Restaurants	723
Portland	429	Germany	783	Beer	675
Boston	403	United Kingdom	692	Recipes & Cooking	533
Austin	395	Canada	580	Vegetarian & Vegan	391

Figure 7.20 TweetDeck Directory

Figure 7.21 NutShellMail

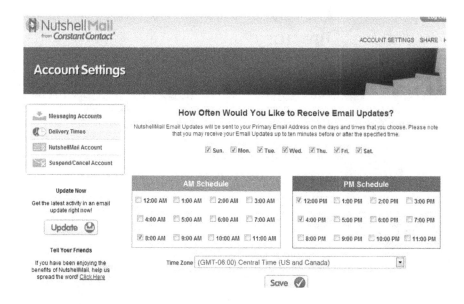

Figure 7.22 NutShellMail delivery times settings

MONITORING YOUR EFFORTS

Google Alerts

Google Alerts is a free service that allows you to setup alerts that match your term search. You can setup these terms for your name, your company and even your competitors, or phrases such as "green living." This is a great tool to keep up to date with your competition, your industry, the news and interesting entertainment opportunities and find out what others may be saying about you, your product or service.

Google will email you when it finds new results for the terms you set. The results can be web pages, newspaper articles or blogs. You could even use these sources to develop your own blog posts or reference as tweets. Learn more and setup your alerts at *http://www.google.com/alerts*.

Google Analytics

Google Analytics is a very powerful web analytics solution. And, yes, like the other tools discussed, it's free for your use. It provides you with lots of rich details about your website traffic and marketing effectiveness. You can receive a detailed report of your site traffic analysis on a daily, weekly, monthly or quarterly basis.

The insights on your website include the number of visitors, total unique visitors, average page views, length of time your visitors remained on your site, search engines used by your visitors, country or territory from where you received site visits, keywords used to get to your web pages, and *bounce rate* of your pages.

Bounce rate is the percentage of visitors who click on your website based on a query search results returned by the search engine and leave your site without reading further because they did not find relevant information. Therefore, bounce rates are affected by the intention of the searchers. Nonetheless, the lower the bounce rate, the better.

You can improve your bounce rate through content—by having *relevant* and ample content. A bounce rate of 40 to 50 percent is generally okay though. One at 30 to 40 percent is better. A bounce rate that's lower than 30 percent is great.

Woopra

Woopra was unveiled in March 2008 and quickly made the news in GeekBrief, TechCrunch, Mashable, and thousands of other sites that brought millions of visitors overnight. Woopra is a *live* tracking and analytics software that is currently running on more than 100,000 websites. I was fortunate to personally interview John Podzadsides at OpenCamp Dallas who explained the features of Woopra. Watch my interview at *http://www.socialexecs.com/blog/interview-with-john-p-on-*

woopra.

Woopra lets you keep track of visitors coming, going and moving through your site *as* these activities take place. To setup your account visit *http://www.woopra.com.*

Basic Steps to Becoming Socially-Savvy

Following is a list of the basic items you need in your social media toolbox:

1. **Google Email.** You will need your Gmail account for various applications including YouTube, Google Analytics, RSS Feeds, and other Google tools of which you may want to take advantage. To set up your Google email log on to *http://mail.gmail.com.*

2. **Yahoo Email.** You need to have a Yahoo email set up to create your Flickr account. To set up your Yahoo email account log on to *http://mail.yahoo.com.*

3. **Google Public Profile.** This is your online business card (well, a bit better than that). This profile enables you to provide a brief bio about you, upload your photo, add a little bit of personality and include links to your website and social media sites. To setup your Google profile, follow the simple steps by logging on to *http://www.google.com/profiles.* You can view my personal Google profile as an example and a guide to complete your own at

http://www.google.com/profiles/dinalima77#about.

4. **Gravatar.** As Gravatar.com explains, "Your Gravatar is an image that follows you from site to site appearing beside your name when you do things like comment or post on a blog. Avatars help identify your posts on blogs and web forums." To setup your avatar image, log on to *http://www.gravatar.com.* You can also add your avatar when you set up your WordPress blog.

Social Networking Do's

- Feed your blog posts into your networking sites such as Facebook, Twitter, and LinkedIn.

- Reply to comments made on your blog posts in Facebook, Twitter, and LinkedIn in a timely manner.

Social Networking Don'ts:

- Don't always post entries on Facebook and Twitter about your new blog posts. Use these tools to build relationships. Follow the general rule of a 10:1 or 15:1 ratio, where you make 10 (or 15) contributions and engage in conversation, to 1 new reference on your website or new blog post.

- Don't feel that you have to sign up for every single social networking site available. Be selective on your choices and use the ones that make sense for your business.

- Don't feel pressured to become a Facebook fan for every invitation you receive.

8 – FACEBOOK: BUILD RAVING FANS

"Advocacy is the newest kid on the marketing block. While we've always known that people make decisions based on advice from their peers, we've never been able to bake that into a plan the way we have now."

Gary Stein, Vice President of Strategy, Ammo Marketing

With your website and/or blog in place, you will be ready to start delving into the world of social media. I suggest you start with Facebook, Twitter and LinkedIn. With over 500 million users, Facebook is the most widely used social networking platform where you can connect with friends, create events, share videos, share photos and create a Fan Page for your business. I will discuss Twitter and LinkedIn more in depth in Chapters Nine and Ten respectively.

In Chapter Twelve I've included step-by-step guidelines on how to setup your Facebook personal profile and your business fan page. It will be very helpful for you to have these two profiles setup to take advantage of additional tips provided in this chapter.

Here are the essentials and tips for what Facebook profiles need to include:

FACEBOOK

Your Facebook Personal Page

Keep your personal Facebook page personal and share business news with your friends occasionally. Use caution as to what you post on your personal page. If not used wisely, you could damage your professional image. When creating your personal profile include:

- Basic information (current city, hometown, gender, birthday where you can select the option "show only month & day in my profile," your bio, favorite quotations, etc.)

- Photo

- Likes and interests

- Education and work

    o Colleges/universities attended

    o Current and former companies worked for

- Contact Information

    o E-mail addresses

    o Phone numbers

    o URLs for your website, blog, Twitter account, LinkedIn, etc.

Be sure to secure the user name for your personal account at *http://www.facebook.com/username.* For fan pages, Facebook requires that you have a minimum of 25 fans prior to reserving your user name for your business page.

Your Facebook Fan Page

Your Facebook fan page is your business page. It enables you to build a fan base with whom you can communicate on a regular basis. Fans not only communicate with you, but they communicate and help each other as well (see Figure 8.1). Determine your target audience. For example, if you're a home builder, it will be beneficial to build relationships with realtors, those seeking to build, and existing home owners. It may not be advantageous if you build your fan base primarily with other builders.

Seek those that are in your target market, or who are connected to the audience you want to reach, and converse with these individuals. Provide tips and talk about items that would interest your market niche.

Figure 8.1 Facebook fans communicate and help each other in your fan page, which generates more activity

Create a Fan Page

When creating your fan page, choose your category and page name of your business thoughtfully.

Insert Keywords in your Fan Page

Search engines index fan pages. Therefore, consider inserting keywords in your page name. For example,

"Dina Lima | Social Media Consultant, Speaker and Trainer"

"TexasGreenSource.com | Find Local. Buy Local."

Post Videos

Facebook gives you the opportunity to share videos with your friends and fans. Take advantage of this feature to enhance your page. Figure 8.2 shows an example.

 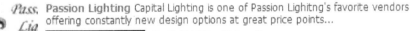 **Passion Lighting** Capital Lighting is one of Passion Lighitng's favorite vendors offering constantly new design options at great price points...

Capital Lighting Fixture Company

www.youtube.com

See the latest home lighting products from one of the leading lighting manufacturers in North America. Take a look at the newest styles from Capital Lighting Fixture Company, and check out their web site ...

April 3 at 10:05pm · Comment · Like · Share

 **Passion Lighting** One of Passion Lighting's newest vendors...great undercabinet, specialty, and LED holiday lighting systems...

American Lighting, Inc.

www.youtube.com

See the latest home lighting products from one of the leading lighting manufacturers in North America. Take a look at the newest styles from American Lighting, Inc. and check out their web site at www.americanlighting.com to find your local American Lighting Association retail showroom.

April 3 at 10:03pm · Comment · Like · Share

Figure 8.2 Post videos on your Facebook fan page

Post Special Content

Take advantage of creating special announcements. You can do this as a post entry directly on your wall. You never know how that accomplishment can get you new business! Figure 8.3 exemplifies how sharing special announcements can ignite a new sale. You can also create a separate tab for special content, although this will require knowledge of FBML, a programming language very similar to HTML. Figure 8.4 provides an example of an attractive advertisement in a separate tab.

Figure 8.3 Sharing your successes could get you new business (view the second comment)

Figure 8.4 Special announcement tab

Find Fans

Before you start asking people to become your fans, add some content to your page. Most people will take a look at your content before becoming fans. There are a few ways that you can invite friends, customers and prospects to fan your page:

1. **Suggest to friends**

   o Click the "Suggest to Friends" link that appears below your profile logo or photo on the upper left hand corner of your fan page. See Figure 8.5.

   o You will get a pop-up window that displays all your friends profile photos. Click on the friends that you'd like to suggest your fan page to. You will only be able to click on those friends who are not yet fans of your page.

Figure 8.5 "Suggest to Friends" link on your Facebook Fan Page appears underneath your uploaded logo

2. **Post an invitation on your personal profile wall**

   o Click the "Share" button located below your fans photos on left sidebar of your Fan page. The "Post to Profile" pop-up window will appear. Type in your message. Click the "Share" button. See Figure 8.6.

Figure 8.6 "Post to Profile" option to post an invitation on your wall inviting friends to like your fan page

3. **Share via your personal e-mail or Facebook e-mail**

   o Click the "Share" button located on the bottom left of

your Fan page. The "Post to Profile" pop-up window will appear.

o On the "Post to Profile" window, click the link "Send as a Message instead." (See Figure 8.7).

o In the "To" field, type in the name of a friend, list or email address.

o In the "Message" field, type in your message.

o Click the "Send Message" button.

Figure 8.7 "Send as a Message" option to send direct invitations to friends to like your fan page

Set Fan Page Administrators

You can set other individuals to manage your fan page. Here's how to do it:

• Click the "Edit Page" link that appears below your profile logo or photo on the upper left hand corner of your fan page.

- Scroll down and in the middle of the page you will see the section labeled "Admins". Your photo should appear there as the current administrator.

- Click on the "Add" button to add other administrators.

Promote Your Facebook Fan Page

Promote your Fan page on your website, blog, e-mail signature, e-mail campaigns, Facebook personal page, your business cards and other collateral material. Don't forget to include a "Follow us on Facebook" button in a visible location of your website.

Facebook Do's

- Use your real name and photo.
- Complete your biography.
- Use the month and day only for your birth date, for security reasons. You can also choose not to display your birth date.
- Join groups.
- Consider what you share and the tone in which you share it.
- Engage in conversation with others and post comments.
- Think before you reply to negative comments. Maintain your

professionalism.

Facebook Don'ts

- Don't announce where you're going!
- Don't share personal information. Protect your privacy.
- Don't make negative comments. The world is listening. Only share what you would feel comfortable sharing with Grandma!
- Don't post photographs, postings or comments that could hinder your image with prospective clients, business partners or employers.
- Don't post anything if you're not up to it or are having a bad day.
- Don't hit "reply all" in group emails.
- Don't feel the pressure of having to befriend everyone or join every imaginable group. Be selective.
- Don't set up your business as a person.
- Don't use Facebook as a selling field or self-promotion. Focus on building relationships.

9 – TWITTER: ATTRACT LOYAL FOLLOWERS

"Engage rather than sell... Work as a co-creator, not a marketer."
Tom H. C. Anderson, Market Researcher

Micro-blogging is a term described by Wikipedia as a passive broadcast medium in the form of blogging. A microblog differs from a traditional blog in that its content is typically much smaller, in both actual size and aggregate file size. A microblog entry could consist of nothing but a short sentence fragment, an image or embedded video.

Twitter is a micro-blogging tool that lets you send messages to the world in just 140 characters. Some ways to build a following is by sharing informative links, answering questions and re-tweeting others' tweets. Twitter has experienced phenomenal growth. With Twitter having roughly 20 million unique visitors[1] each month and with your opportunity to be part (and beneficiary) of this huge internet phenomenon, having your Twitter presence will help your personal and business branding. Think of Twitter as your customer relationship management system.

Because Twitter restricts your message to 140 characters, use a URL shortener, such as *http://bit.ly* or *http://tinyurl.com*, when referencing URL's on your tweets. However, HootSuite has an embedded URL shortener. To set up your Twitter account, follow the step-by-step guide in Chapter Thirteen.

WHAT DO YOU TWEET?

Anything you'd like! But don't miss the opportunity to show yourself resourceful to your Twitter network of followers. Figures 9.1 through 9.4 provide some examples of various kinds of tweets.

Figure 9.1 Tweet about a new product, inform or inspire

Figure 9.2 Tweet about specials you're offering

Figure 9.3 Tweet thank you notes to your followers

Figure 9.4 Tweet with a little personality

TWITTER LINGO

Tweet. A message you post on Twitter.

ReTweet (RT). When you send a tweet from another user. As you scroll over a tweet post, Twitter gives you the option to "Reply" or "Retweet." Select the "Retweet" option if you want to share a tweet from another user (see Figure 9.5).

Hash Tag. This is the pound sign (#) that helps to categorize tweets, search for a particular topic, and track trends.

User Name. The name for your Twitter account, i.e., @yourname this is up to 14 characters in length. When referencing your user name, use the @yourname format.

Direct Messaging (DM): this takes place when you send a direct message to another Twitter user. To do this you add a "D" and a space before a Twitter user name. Some Twitter users dislike DM's and may indicate that in their bio. Figure 9.6 provides an example of a Direct Message.

Figure 9.5 Retweet and Reply options

Figure 9.6 Example of a Direct Message

WHO TO FOLLOW

Follow friends, business colleagues and associates, business leaders, people you meet, and people you admire. Your network is a collection of intelligence, expertise and advice. The more people with whom you're engaged, the more opportunities you'll have to get information that can benefit your business. Use Twitter to share and receive.

SEARCH FOR FOLLOWERS

Start by searching for your friends and colleagues. Another great source is to browse through the suggested users provided by Twitter. When you logon to your Twitter account, click on "Find People" menu option, and select the "Browse Suggestions" tab. Twitter users exist in various categories. Go through the categories and choose the ones you like. There are no guarantees that the Twitterers you follow will follow you back. Some of the users may do so. Figure 9.7 provides a view of Twitter's suggested users.

Twellow.com is great source to consider when finding people to follow. Twellow is your Twitter yellow pages. Learn more at *http://www.twellow.com/*.

Tweepz, *http://tweepz.com*, use it to find matching profiles of people you wish to follow. See Figure 9.8.

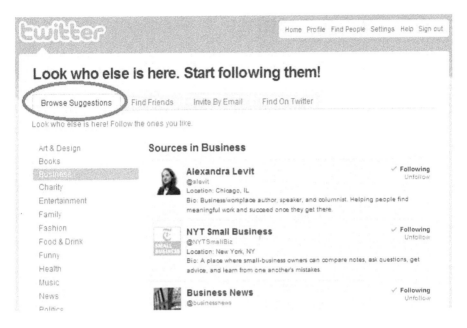

Figure 9.7 Twitter suggested users

Figure 9.8 Tweepz.com lets you find matching profiles

COMPLETE YOUR PROFILE

Use your brief Bio section to tell a little bit about yourself. Keep it short, sweet and don't miss the opportunity to add a bit of personality. People love to connect with real people. Figure 9.9 shows a couple of Twitter bio examples.

Name Dina Lima
Location Hurst, TX
Web http://www.DinaLi...
Bio Soccer Mom, Social Media Strategist, Green Home Educator, WordPress Developer, Love tea, chocolate, Italian & Mexican cuisine, classical music and quietude

Name Michael Garabedian
Location Southlake, Texas (D/FW)
Web http://www.garabe...
Bio Disney Fan who builds luxury homes in Southlake & Westlake, Texas, Computer Geek, Bike Rider, Diet Coke & Snickers For Breakfast, NO MLMs, Don't DM/Spam Me, DU

Figure 9.9 Twitter bio examples

CUSTOMIZE THE TWITTER BACKGROUND

Customizing your Twitter background is important to creating a cohesive branding throughout multiple social networking platforms. Have your background designed to complement your website or blog. A recommended size for your background graphic is 2048 pixels by 1707 pixels, which would showcase well on most standard size monitors. Some of the information to add on the top left corner of your graphic includes: your logo, photo (if applicable), and contact information such as your website, e-mail address and phone number. Even though your website and e-mail addresses are not hot links in your Twitter background image, it is a good practice to include them for people to know how to learn more about you. See Figures 9.10 and 9.11.

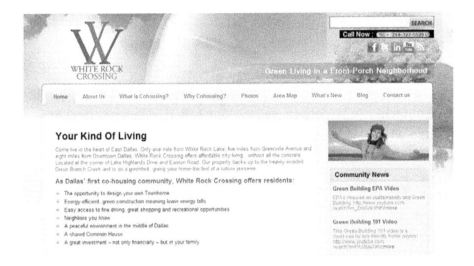

Figure 9.10 Main website

Figure 9.11 Customized Twitter background

PROMOTE TWITTER

Promote your Twitter @username on your website, blog, e-mail signature, e-mail campaigns, Facebook personal and fan pages, your business cards and other collateral material. Consider including a "Follow us on Twitter" button on a visible location of your website, e-mail blasts or e-zines.

When tweeting, focus on building relationships. Remember that none of us like to be sold to, yet we love to buy! The best thing to do is observe what and how others are tweeting and then try it yourself. As you get your feet wet, you will find your own rhythm.

LINK TWITTER AND FACEBOOK

Link your Facebook fan page to your business Twitter account where your Facebook entries will be generated as tweets automatically. You can follow the steps to link your accounts at *http://www.facebook.com/twitter*.

If you only have set up one Twitter username, then link your Facebook fan page to it. If you have a separate Twitter username for your business, then link your Facebook fan page to it. This will give you the freedom to keep your personal Twitter account only for personal use.

Twitter Do's

- Choose a name that makes sense and complete your profile.
- Monitor your Twitter conversations using tools like

TweetDeck and HootSuite. Use TwitterCounter.com to analyze statistics on your account.

- Tweet about what is happening now, not 30 days ago.
- Provide tips, share news, re-tweet others' contents, ask questions, include links to good articles or videos and link back to your website or blog when you post new content.
- Keep a balance on your message: use a 10:1 or 15:1 ratio, where you make contributions and talk about other things 10 to 15 times, and post news about your service or new blog post on your site 1 time. Be sensitive when tweeting about your business.
- Follow those people you want following you such as great Twitter players, the influential Twitterers that have many followers. **TIP:** if you discover a great leader that has lots of followers, follow them first. Check out their website, find something positive to say from whatever you read on their website and send them an email. Mention in your note that you are following them on Twitter and that you wish for them to connect with you as well. Don't say in your note "I want you to follow me too!" Be tactful. Your positive note could be enough to encourage them to follow you in return. By being part of their network, you may pick up some of their followers to follow you as well.
- Re-tweet others' interesting tweets; ask questions and be a part of conversations.
- Spend time following a number of people. Watch and learn how they communicate so that you can get in the communication flow more effectively.
- Respond to direct messages if you receive them. This can help you build followers.
- Thank those who follow you.

- Avoid boring tweets. Be purposeful, authentic and transparent. Always think about the image you want to portray.
- Be professional even when negative comments come your way. Keep your cool and respond appropriately.
- Include the words "New Post" followed by the title when you wish to share a new post you've written. Include a direct link to your post on your blog or website.
- Share links to other articles or sources you find interesting that can benefit the people in your network. Use URL shortening tools for the URL links.
- Set up specific times in your daily or weekly schedule to tweet and maintain the balance with other major responsibilities. This will help you be consistent, stay organized and preserve your sanity!

Twitter Don'ts

- Don't announce where you're going!
- Don't share personal information. Protect your privacy.
- Don't tweet if you're not up to it or are having a rough day.
- Don't use Twitter as a selling field or self-promotion.

10 – LINKEDIN: MAKE DYNAMIC BUSINESS CONNECTIONS

"It isn't just what you know, and it isn't just who you know. It's actually who you know, who knows you, and what you do for a living."

Bob Burg, Speaker and Co-author of *The Go-Giver*

Each time I teach a seminar I ask the attendees how many of them have their LinkedIn profile setup. Normally about half of the attendees raise their hand. Then when I ask part two of my question, as to how many of them have their LinkedIn profile 100 percent complete, almost everyone's hands go down as they chuckle!

It is important to have your LinkedIn profile complete. And with additional applications available, it is easy to enhance your profile and make the maximum use of LinkedIn's capabilities.

LinkedIn is where you connect with other professionals and business people. It is your online Rolodex and résumé. Use LinkedIn to build your personal brand, network and create strategic business alliances.

Complete Your Profile

Have your résumé open when you get ready to complete your profile. Figure 10.1 provides an example of a completed LinkedIn profile. Include the following information:

- Name

- Photo

- Title

- Location

- Industry

- Bio (executive bio)

- Specialties

- Current and past employers

- Education

- Websites (company website, blog, personal website, Facebook page, Facebook fan page)

- Your Twitter username

- Public Profile name (edit it to assign a direct name to your profile; example: *http://www.linkedin.com/in/dinalima*)

- E-mail address

Make Connections

Here are several ways to grow your LinkedIn connections:

- Use the search function to find colleagues from previous employments, people with whom you currently do business, or people with the similar interests as you, and send them a personal note with your invitation to be connected.

- Invite new people you meet at networking events.

- Get introduced to others' connections by using the "Get introduced through a connection" function in LinkedIn.

- Go through the business cards you have collected.

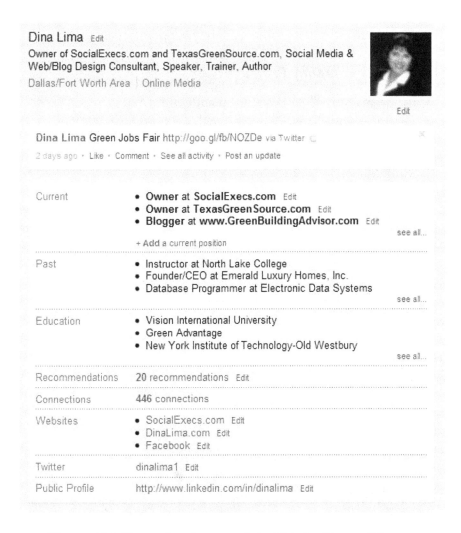

Figure 10.1 Example of a completed LinkedIn profile

Get Recommendations

Request recommendations from your clients, colleagues, previous managers, business associates and people with whom you do or have done business. Endorsements help increase your credibility and visibility. Don't forget to send a thank you note to those who take the time to endorse you and your work. When you accept a recommendation, LinkedIn also gives you the option to return the favor. Be sure to endorse others as they send you their requests.

Create Your Company Profile

Company profiles provide useful information to clients and anyone interested in learning more about your company. Figure 10.2 displays an example of a LinkedIn company profile.

Your company profile should include:

- Company name
- Logo
- Locations
- Company Blog
- Company Biography
- Specialties
- Website URL
- Industry
- Type of company (public company, privately held, partnership, etc.)
- Status
- Number of employees
- Year founded

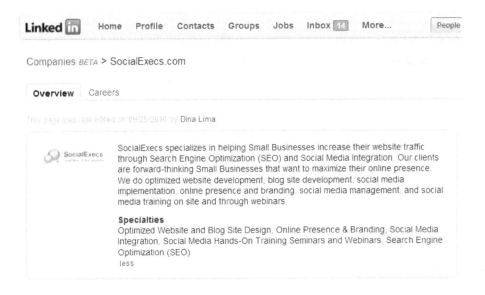

Figure 10.2 A completed LinkedIn company profile

Join Groups

Use the search function in the "Group Directory" to join groups that focus on your interests. Groups help you interact with others, share ideas and even request feedback on a question you may have. Groups can be a great source of professional intelligence and an oasis of great ideas. You can also create your own group and build your own network. Figure 10.3 displays the search results for groups related to "green building." Notice the "Create a Group" button below the "Search Groups" box.

Post Jobs

The Jobs section of LinkedIn enables you to post available jobs in your organization. For individuals, looking for work is made simple via the "Search for Jobs" function. For businesses, LinkedIn is an excellent tool to recruit quality people as their online résumé, activity, and recommendations from peers and past employers are found in one location, making your recruitment process more effective. Posting jobs is a paid service. You can save a ton of money on heavy ad or agency costs when you can use this connection tool.

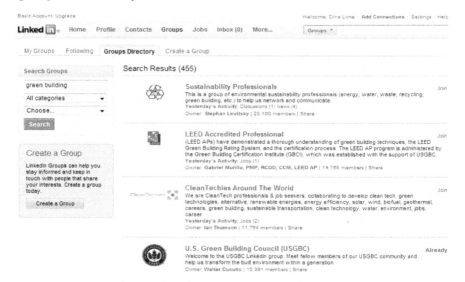

Figure 10.3 LinkedIn Groups Directory search results

Post Events

The Events section of LinkedIn allows you to post and join events. This is an excellent way to promote to your classes, seminars, networking events, webinars, etc. See an example in Figure 10.4.

Tap into the Power of LinkedIn Answers

"LinkedIn Answers" is a powerful tool to get feedback, tips, advice, and opinions from the brains your network. Sometimes you will get answers from people outside your network. Participate in answering questions to showcase your expertise (see Figure 10.5). Access LinkedIn Answers from the "More…" menu option and select "Answers" from the pull-down selections.

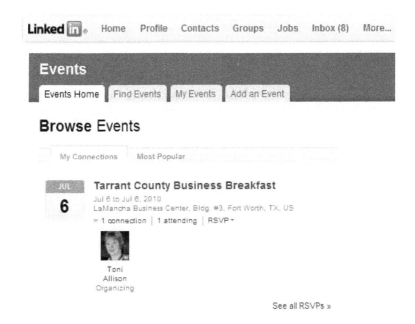

Figure 10.4 Example of Events page in LinkedIn

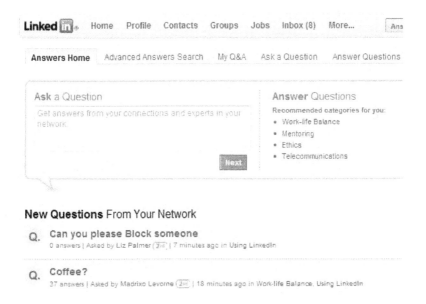

Figure 10.5 LinkedIn Answers page

Combine Other Applications

LinkedIn has a great variety of applications of which you can take advantage to enhance your profile and maximize the use of this platform. From your LinkedIn "More..." menu option select "Application Directory" for a list of supported apps. Here's a quick list of the various applications supported by LinkedIn:

- **WordPress**. Links to your blog and displays your recent posts.

- **Blog Link**. Connect your blog to your profile (supports WordPress and Typad).

- **Tweets**. View the latest tweets from your network and post your tweets, which you can also choose to share with your LinkedIn network.

- **Company Buzz**. See tweets about your company.

- **SlideShare Presentations and Google Presentations**. Share your presentations online.

- **Polls**. Get information from your connections on a particular topic.

- **Events**. Find professional events such as local meet-ups or seminars, and learn which events your connections are attending.

- **Huddle Workspaces**. Work on projects with your connections in a private, secure online workspace.

- **Box.net Files**. Manage various types of files online and share them with your friends and colleagues.

- **Reading List by Amazon**. Share with others what you're reading.

- **MyTravel**. Used to share your travel schedule with your network.

LinkedIn Do's

- Secure your URL. Edit your URL by clicking the "Edit" link in the "Public Profile" section of your profile that appears below your websites and Twitter sections (see Figure 10.1).

- Complete your profile 100 percent.

- Provide details about your work and the things you do.

- Update your status at least once per week.

- Join relevant groups that align with your interests.

- Write recommendations and make requests for recommendations.

- Answer questions.

- Take advantage of using available applications. Find applications under the "More…" menu option and click on "Application Directory".

LinkedIn Don'ts

- Don't forget to update your status at least once per week.

- Don't feel obligated to give an introduction.

- Don't feel pressured to reply to endorsement requests.

- Don't forward questionable requests to your connections.

11 – READY, SET, GO!

"The ability to concentrate and to use time well is everything."
Lee Iacocca, American Businessman

Social media is not a one-size-fits-all solution. Reviewing your needs and audience will help you plan the right social media marketing mix for your business. A planned and sound social media strategy is the key to building your network of current and potential customers, engaging your past clients for additional and future referrals, and attracting new visitors to your site through search engine optimization (SEO) and social media optimization (SMO).

Here are some essentials that managing your social media requires:

- **Commitment**. If you start it, keep it up.

- **Consistency**. If you commit to writing a blog once per week or month, stick to it. Schedule author time slots just like you would a doctor's appointment.

- **People skills**. Be courteous and build rapport.

- **Customer service skills**. Be attentive to your clients' concerns.

- **Maintenance and planning**. Manage your online branding.

You see the value of incorporating social media into your

business. So how do you get started? There's two ways to go about it, namely, doing it yourself, or finding help.

If you are a hands-on entrepreneur and decide that doing things yourself makes the most sense, the good news is that most of the social media tools are easy to learn and navigate through. There is only one major issue: they require time. Prepare a monthly schedule to help you stay on track. Be disciplined in following through with your game plan.

If you are the visionary type of business owner that likes to focus on the direction and growth of your business, then you'll find that the most viable solution is to hire the experts to take care of the detailed technical aspects of social media setup and/or its continued management. Larger businesses have seen the value of social media to the point that they have created social media management departments. Other smaller businesses find it beneficial to outsource this important activity. By outsourcing it, you eliminate additional expenses entailed with hiring employees, such as payroll taxes, insurance and other fringe benefits.

As you create a game plan for your business, there are several key questions noted below that are essential to help in creating a viable strategy.

TOP 7 QUESTIONS TO PLAN YOUR STRATEGY

Review the following questions with your business partners, brainstorm them with your key employees or managers, or share them with your social media consultant. Your answers to these critical questions will provide a clear roadmap to accomplish your goals.

1. **What do you hope to gain from your social media presence?**

   - Identify your objectives.

   - Set specific goals.

2. **Do you know how your customers want to engage with you?**

   - Find out by researching your audience.

   - Use methods that resonate with your audience.

   - Determine which communities should you join (Twitter, Facebook, other?) and be active in them.

3. **Which existing staff members are best qualified to support the effort?**

   Who from your staff is capable to:

   - initiate the conversation with your audience?

   - remain engaged and provide tips, advice, solutions to questions or comments?

   - educate your current and future customers about your products or services?

   - generate enthusiasm about what you offer your target market?

     TIP: If there are several people in your office who come to mind, create a blogging schedule where the load can be shared. If you don't feel that you can be responsible for these efforts and don't have an internal person that is enthusiastic about it, consider outsourcing it.

4. **How much will you budget for the effort?**

   - Interactive tools are free to use but they require time and energy. In business, time equals money.

   - Prepare for expenses to maximize the use of social media marketing tools.

   - If properly planned, you can enjoy greater savings rather than using traditional methods only.

   - Depending on your business, you may need to do a

combination of traditional and online marketing activities.

5. **What is your plan for integration?**

- Complement your current marketing program.

- Promote your social networking accounts on your website, e-mail signatures, e-mail campaigns, e-newsletters, business cards, flyers and other collateral material.

- Be consistent across all platforms.

- Determine how your current public relations and marketing programs will be involved with your social media efforts.

- Maintain all your programs synchronized.

6. **How will you measure your success or failure?**

Will you measure by:

- Increase in number of followers/fans?

- Increase in website traffic?

- Positive or increased feedback?

- New or more referrals?

- Revenue growth?

- Mentions on other sites?

7. **If you Google your name or company name right now, will you be happy with the results?**
- Do you have a blog?
- Is your LinkedIn profile 100% complete?
- Do you have your Facebook personal page and Fan Page and are you engaged?
- Do you have your Twitter account?
- Do you have your Google Profile complete?

Keeping Up with the Pace of Social Media

- Set up search terms in Google Alerts. You can access the tool at *http://www.google.com/alerts*.

- Sign up for e-zines that specialize and provide social media tips on a regular basis.

- Stay in touch with social media news sites. Some of the most popular are:

  - *www.copyblogger.com*

  - *www.digitalbuzzblog.com*

  - *www.emarketer.com*

  - *www.mashable.com*

  - *www.readwriteweb.com*

  - *www.socialmediaexaminer.com*

  - *www.socialmediaprofs.com*

  - *www.techcrunch.com*

  - *www.web-strategist.com*

- Use TweetDeck to learn about what your network is tweeting. You'll come across great links to articles, news, and new products.

- Stay alert about new technologies that people in your network share. One of the Twitter users in my network posted a tweet on this new free service called *www.Twylah.com* which creates a personally branded blog out of your tweets, automatically!

- Another great service is *www.ObjectiveMarketer.com*. This is a paid service and is an excellent tool if you're seeking a more sophisticated management of your social media activity.

SECTION II – SOCIAL MEDIA 9-1-1 QUICK START-UP GUIDE

"Definiteness of purpose is the starting point of all achievement."

W. Clement Stone, Businessman, Philanthrophist and Author

12 – FACEBOOK STARTUP GUIDE

SETUP YOUR FACEBOOK PERSONAL PROFILE

1. Log on to *http://www.facebook.com*
2. Enter your information on the home page and click the "Sign Up" button. (You can change your birth date settings to hide your birth year once you're inside your account).

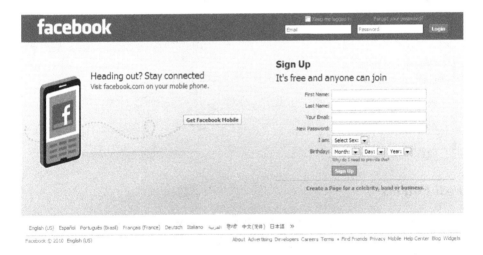

3. Facebook will send you a confirmation email. Click the link included in your Confirmation email to activate your account.

Complete Your Facebook Profile

- Change your photo. Scroll over the Facebook image that appears on the top left corner of the page and click on "Change Picture" link. Follow the instructions to upload your

photo.
- Edit your brief bio below your photo.
- Click on the link "Edit My Profile" below your uploaded picture to edit your profile. You can also click on the "Info" tab.
- Click the "Edit Information" link to edit your profile information.

- Click on each of the sections noted below to complete your profile. To save changes, click on "Done Editing" button.

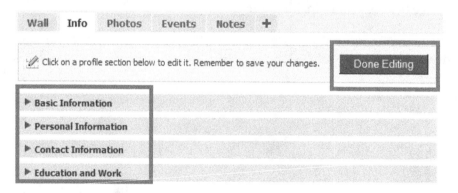

Post Entries

- There's a couple of ways to post entries: from your News Feed page and from your Profile page.
- By default when you logon you'll be brought to the News Feed page. To get to it, you can also click on the "Home" option on the top right menu from inside Facebook.

- On the News Feed page click on the link "Status" which will make the box status visible. Type your message and click on the "Share" button.

- On the Profile page, which you get to by clicking on the "Profile" option on the top right menu from inside Facebook, click on "Status". Type your message and click on "Share" to publish your entry.

- To include a URL link simply copy and paste the URL on your entry. When you do, Facebook will automatically pick up the details of your URL and give you options for the "thumbnail" photo. In the following screen, it shows that there are five photos available to choose from. Make your selection and click on the "Share" button to post your entry.

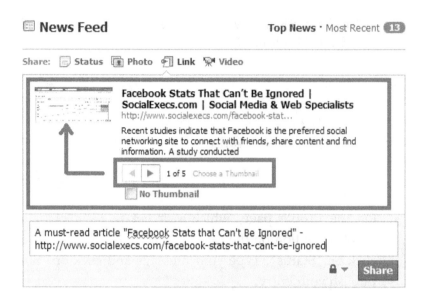

Add Friends

- Enter the name of the person you wish to be friends with in the Search box, which will appear on the top left corner on the top menu bar inside Facebook.

- As you begin to type the first name, Facebook will begin to show you a list of people whose name begins with the letters you're typing.
- Select the person you want to friend from the search results. Facebook will take you to that person's Profile page.
- Click the "Add as Friend" button on the person's profile and the "Add Friend" window will pop up.

- To add a personal message in your invitation, click "Add a personal message..." from the "Add Friend" window and type in your message. Sometimes this is helpful to remind people of how you both met in the past.

- You can also add people to different categories to organize your list of friends.

- Click the "Send Request" button. When the person accepts your request, you will then be friends.
- If the person you're friending has made their Profile public, you'll be able to see the friends and also send them an invitation as well.

Reserve Your Alias Name

- To reserve your alias go to *http://www.facebook.com/username*. This will create a direct link to your personal Facebook page, i.e., *http://www.facebook.com/yourname*.

CREATE YOUR FACEBOOK BUSINESS PAGE

Your Facebook business page is an essential part of your online marketing plan. To create a business fan page you must first have a personal profile created. Once you have created your personal profile, you will then be able to create your business page. For clarity purposes a "fan" page or "business" page are one in the same.

CAUTION: the original administrator who sets up your Facebook business page will be the person with full access to manage the page. Remember that business pages are setup under a personal Facebook account. Therefore, I highly recommend that you have your business page setup under *your* personal Facebook account, rather than an employee who could move on and change company or career. After you have the page setup under your personal Facebook account, you can add other administrators whom you can also delete as it becomes necessary.

Keep in mind that Facebook continues to make changes to the functionality of fan pages. Stay abreast of updates so that you can take full advantage of new features added.

Following are the steps to create your business page.

- Once logged in, locate and click the link "Create a Page". If you cannot locate the link, use the direct URL to this page: *http://www.facebook.com/pages/create.php*.
- Make the appropriate selection for your business page. Your choices are:

- o   Local business
- o   Brand, product, or organization
- o   Artist, band or public figure
- Give your page an effective name by including keywords. For example,

"Dina Lima | Social Media Consultant, Speaker and Trainer" or

"TexasGreenSource.com | Find Local. Buy Local."

- Double check the spelling before you hit the "Create Official Page" button. Luckily, Facebook now allows you to edit your page name.

- Select the appropriate business type:
  - ○ Local business
  - ○ Brand, product or organization
  - ○ Artist, band or public figure
- Select the appropriate category for your business.

- Develop your fan page completely by including:
  - ○ Company logo
    - Upload your logo by scrolling over the top left-hand corner image and when you see the "pencil" icon click on the "change" option

- For cohesive branding purpose, it is a good idea to carry the look and feel of your website into your Facebook presence as well. To that end, have a custom graphic made that mirrors the colors and feel of your website. Use the Facebook supported dimensions of 180 pixels wide and 500 pixels high. You can go up to 200 pixels wide by 587 pixels high. The size for the graphics in my business pages are 200 pixels wide by 500 by pixels high.
  - Website URL
  - Links to your social networking sites
  - Contact information such as your phone number and e-mail
  - Company overview
  - Product or service information
  - Videos about your company, products or services, community involvement, customer testimonials, etc.
  - Photos of your products, projects or other special events, etc.
- To invite friends to join your page, click on "Suggest to Friends" link which appears below your uploaded image on your business page.

Edit Page

Promote with an Ad

Add to My Page's Favorites

Suggest to Friends

- To link your page with your Twitter account, follow the steps at *http://www.facebook.com/twitter*

MANAGE YOUR FACEBOOK BUSINESS PAGE

- To manage your page, logon to your Facebook personal profile.

- Click on the Account pull down menu that appears on the top right corner of the page and select the option "Manage Pages".

- Click on the "Go to Page" button for the page you want to manage. Facebook will take you to the "Wall" section of the page.

- Select the "Edit Page" from the options that appear below your uploaded logo.

- The "Edit Page" option will take you to the "Basic Information" tab by default.

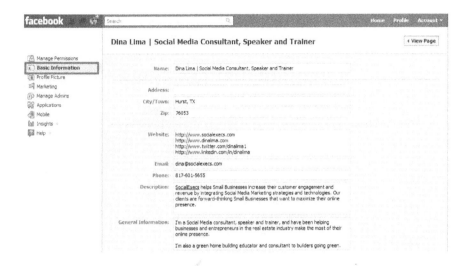

- You can also manage other aspects of your page by clicking the management options:

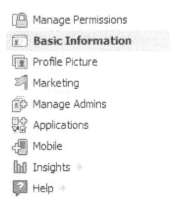

- These are the management options and a brief description of what each of them allow you to do:

    o **Manage Permissions**. Lets you add restrictions as to

who can view the permissions page, country restrictions, age restrictions, default landing tab, and posting ability.

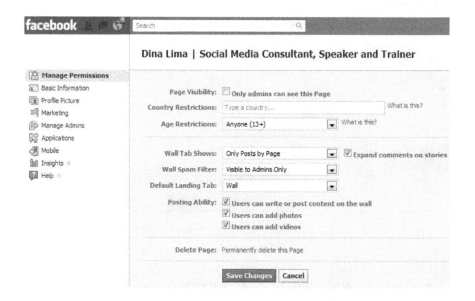

o **Basic Information.** Is where you edit the page name, business address, website(s) URL(s), email, phone number, business description and general information.

TIP: include the full URL reference for your websites.

o **Profile Picture.** Is where you upload your business page profile image.

o **Marketing.** Provides you various options to market your business page including: advertising on Facebook, inviting your fans, getting a Facebook badge, adding a "Like Box" on your site, creating your alias (name for your page, example: *http://facebook.com/dinalimaspeaker*) or sending an update to your fan base.

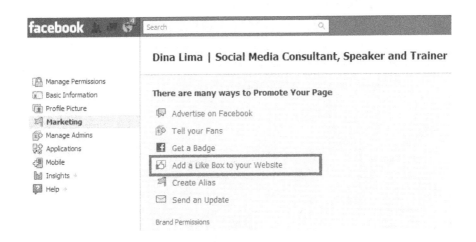

- o **Manage Admins** – is where you add or remove administrators for your business page.

- o **Applications** – lists the applications you've added to your business page, such as YouTube. To view more applications available scroll to the bottom of this page and click on the link "Browse more applications."

- o **Mobile** – if you have email on your mobile phone (such as a Blackberry), Facebook provides you a unique email address to upload messages and photos from your mobile device.

- o **Insights** – provides you statistics on your business page traffic.

RESERVE YOUR ALIAS NAME FOR YOUR FAN PAGE

- To reserve your alias go to *http://www.facebook.com/username* to create a direct link to your Facebook fan page, i.e., *http://www.facebook.com/yourcompany.*

USE FACEBOOK SOCIAL PLUGINS

- Facebook offers various social Plugins. Logon to the developers section for a complete list of all available Plugins *http://developers.facebook.com/plugins.*

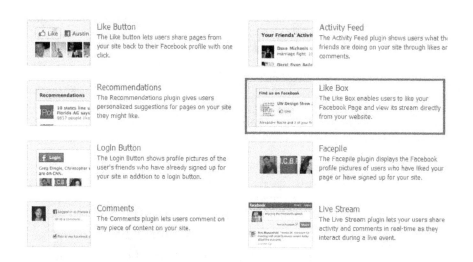

- To add a "Like Box" on your WordPress website, select the "Like Box" Plugin.

- When you get to the "Like Box" Plugin page, enter the direct URL link of your Facebook fan page on the "Facebook Page URL" field, as shown in the screenshot below. You can change the width of the "Like Box" in the "Width" field. Select your "Color Scheme" from the pull down menu. Enter the number of "Connections" to display on your "Like Box". Select "Show stream" and "Show header" options. Click on the "Get Code" button to get the code to be inserted in your selected section of your website.

13 – TWITTER AND TWITTER APPS STARTUP GUIDE

SETUP YOUR TWITTER ACCOUNT

The screenshots noted are provided as a guide. Social networking sites update their platforms and they may not look exactly the same.

Following are the steps to set up your Twitter account.

1. Log on to *http://twitter.com*. The home page will show you the top tweets. You can do a quick search for Tweets that use a particular keyword or phrase straight from the home page. Type in your keyword or phrase in the Search box as shown in the image below. Twitter will provide you real time results for your search.

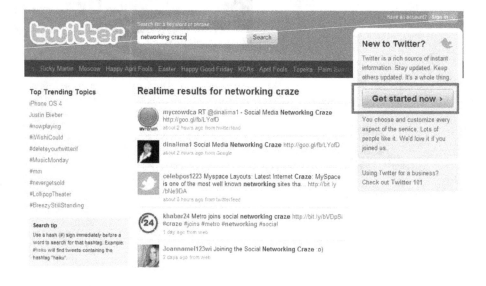

2. To create your Twitter account, click the "Get Started Now" button.
3. Enter all the information requested on the sign up form and click on "Create My Account" button.
4. Twitter will send you a confirmation email. Click the link included in your Confirmation email to activate your account.
5. Twitter will guide you to start following people that are part of your contact list. Twitter checks to see if your contacts have a Twitter account. If they do, you can follow them by following the prompts. You can also find people manually via the "Find People" menu option.

Complete your Twitter profile

1. When you are logged in, go to the "Settings" link from the main menu that appears at the top right-hand corner of the page.

2. Click "Profile" from the sub-menu option.

3. Upload your image, enter your real name, your location, your website address, and a brief bio. Click "Save".
4. Click "Design" from the menu option to choose a different background. Click "Save".

5. Click "Connections" to browse and manage the different Applications that support Twitter (TweetDeck, WordPress, Google, Twitterfeed, LinkedIn, and any new ones that Twitter

adds in the future).

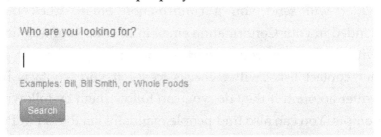

6. Click "Find People" from the top menu.
7. Enter the names of the people you want to find and follow.

8. Once you have found the person you wish to follow, click on the first icon with the plus (+) sign to follow that person.

Customize Your Twitter Background

For cohesive branding, it is good practice to carry the look and feel of your website over to your Twitter background as well. The dimensions for your background should be 2048 pixels wide by 1707 pixels high. This size will fit most large monitors. Have a professional graphics designer do this for you. Include your logo, photo (if applicable) and contact information on the top left-hand corner of the image.

Check out some additional tips on customizing your Twitter background at *http://mashable.com/2009/05/23/twitter-backgrounds*.

Shorten URLs

Because you have a limited number of characters to share your message, you need to use a URL shortening software such as *www.Bitly.com* or *www.TinyURL.com*.

To shorten a URL, logon to *www.Bitly.com* and enter the URL in the box. Click the "Shorten" button.

Your shortened URL will appear as shown in the screen below. Copy and paste on your tweet.

SETUP YOUR TWEETDECK ACCOUNT

TweetDeck is a free application for Twitter that allows you to organize, update, and essentially handle all the @replies, direct messages, re-tweets, and updates that come up 24/7.

TweetDeck is an excellent tool to find new connections. Use the search box to enter keywords relevant to your interests (i.e., "green building", "solar power", "green energy", etc.). TweetDeck will pull up the list of the Twitter users that have the same interests based on the keyword you entered. This helps you to narrow down the list of movers and shakers you want to connect with.

1. Logon to *http://www.tweetdeck.com*. Click the link "Sign In – Register"

2. Sign in using your Twitter Account. Click on the "Sign in with Twitter" button.

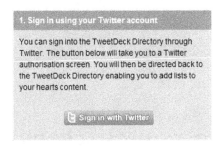

3. Click the "Allow" button to allow TweetDeck Directory access.

SETUP YOUR HOOTSUITE ACCOUNT

HootSuite is one of the best tools you'll come to love because it will help you manage your Twitterati more effectively. HootSuite is a free application for Twitter that allows you administer multiple Twitter profiles, pre-schedule tweets, and measure your success. This tool gives you a lot of control. You can make it a point to schedule your tweets to be posted on your account whenever you want and however often you desire.

1. Logon to *http://hootsuite.com*. Click on the "Sign up Now" button.
2. Create your account. Enter all the requested information. Click "Create Account".

hootsuite

sign up

Create Your Account

Email Address: *

Confirm Email Address: *

Your Name: *

Password: *

Confirm Password: *

Create HootSuite Account

Add Social Networks

Start Managing!

3. Enter your Twitter Login and Password. Click "Add".

4. Add other twitter accounts, or click Finish.

5. Check the email HootSuite sent you. Copy and paste the code in the email in the box noted below. Click "Confirm".

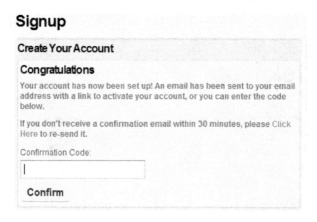

6. Logon to your account.

7. Navigate through the Dashboard's menu options to familiarize yourself with the different functions you can take advantage of.
   • Click on your Twitter User Name on the top tab.

The screen will display:

• Home Feed
• Mentions
• Direct Messages
• Pending Tweets
• The default selection is "Streams" that displays all the Twitter streams. The following buttons appear at the bottom of your screen.

• "Stats" displays all your stats if any.
• "Settings" displays your account settings which you can edit, your social networks, and users.
• "People" displays all your followers.

8. Scheduling Tweets
   • Select "Send Later" option that appears at the top of the page.

- Your screen will then look like this, which will let you schedule your tweets:

- Enter your tweet. Enter the URL if applicable and select "Shrink it". Select the date and time. Click "Schedule". The shortened URL will appear on your message.

- Back on your Dashboard, your scheduled tweets will be displayed.

SETUP AUTORESPONDER

SocialOomph.com, formerly known as TweetLater.com, focuses on productivity solutions for users of today's popular social networks including, Twitter, Facebook, Ping and others. SocialOomph offers free and paid services to help you manage your social presence from setting up autoresponders, scheduling and publishing blog posts and pages, to finding quality friends to follow using keywords. The autoresponder service for Twitter is free of charge and one of the best services in the market.

1. Log on to SocialOomph's website and register a new account, *https://www.socialoomph.com/register*.

2. From the "Social Accounts" menu, select "Add New Account". You'll note that Twitter, Buzz and StatusNet are offered free of charge. You can upgrade to include the other supported networks.

Main Landing Page		
Schedule New Update		
Schedule Blog Post		
Shorten URL		
Statistics ▸		
Social Accounts ▸	Add New Account ▸	Add Twitter
Blogs ▸	Manage Accounts	Add Buzz
Scheduled Updates ▸	Extended Profiles	Add Facebook
Direct Messages ▸	Edit Automation	Add Blog
Followers/Friends ▸	Edit Welcome DM ▸	Add StatusNet
Monitors ▸	Automation Stats	Add Ping.fm
Banner Auctions	Delegate Accounts	Add Blog Feed

3. To send an automatic welcome message each time a new follower follows you on Twitter, check the box "Automatically send a welcome message to new followers."

4. Type in your message in the "Message" box.

5. If you'd like to automatically follow the persons who follow you, check the box "Automatically follow people (new followers) who follow e from this point forward." You're done!

Optional Twitter Account Automation

Auto Welcome:	☑ Automatically send a welcome message to new followers.
Send This Message:	How to rotate welcome messages (and why you should).
	Thank you for the follow! Feel honored... hope that my thoughts/tips/links bring you great value. Find Social Media tips at SocialExecs.com and inspiration at DinaLima.com
	171 characters entered.
Auto Follow:	☑ Automatically follow people (new followers) who follow me from this point forward.
Vet Followers:	☐ Place the automation of a new follower on hold for three days so that I can manually approve or reject the action.

14 – LINKEDIN STARTUP GUIDE

SETUP YOUR LINKEDIN ACCOUNT

1. Log on to *http://www.linkedIn.com*.
2. **Complete your profile.**
   Provide the following information:
   - Name
   - Photo
   - Title (enrich it with keywords such as "Owner, SocialExecs.com providing SEO and Social Media Management to Small Businesses"; keep in mind that the maximum length is 120 characters)
   - Location
   - Industry
   - Bio (executive bio)
   - Specialties
   - Current and past employers (describe the work you did in a succinct manner)
   - Education (universities/colleges/trade schools attended)
   - Websites (your company website, blog, personal website, Facebook page, Facebook fan page)
   - Your Twitter account (Username only without the "@" sign)
   - Public Profile name (edit it to assign a direct name to your profile; example: *http://www.linkedin.com/in/dinalima*)
   - E-mail address

3. **Make connections**.

-   Use the search function to find colleagues from previous employments, people you currently do business with, or people with the similar interests as you, and send them a personal note with your invitation.

-   Use the "Advanced People Search" function for additional parameters by clicking the "Advanced" link on the search box that appears on the top right hand-corner of your screen.
-   Once you're in the person's profile, simply click on the link that reads "Add [name] to your network" to send them an invitation to connect.

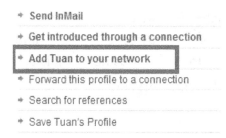

-   Click the "Get introduced through a connection" option to get introduced to someone you don't know personally but would like to have in your professional network.

4. **Get recommendations**.
    -   To request recommendations from peers and past managers, select the "Profile" option and choose "Recommendations" from the drop-down menu.

- Click on the "Request Recommendations" tab.
- Follow the 3-step process to request an endorsement.

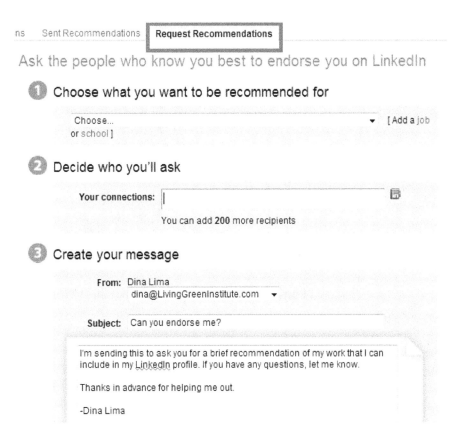

5. **Create your company profile**.
    * To create your company profile, select "Companies" from the main menu.

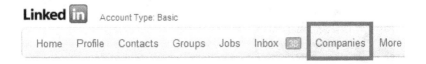

    * Click on the link "Add a Company" link that will appear below the search box at the top right-hand side of the page.

    * Follow the screens to complete your profile. You'll be entering the following information:

        o Company name
        o Logo
        o Locations
        o Company Blog
        o Company Biography
        o Specialties
        o Website URL
        o Industry
        o Type of company (public company, partnership, etc.)
        o Status
        o Number of employees
        o Year founded

6. **Join groups**.
    * To find groups to join, select the "Groups" option from the

main menu and choose "Groups Directory" from the drop-down selections.

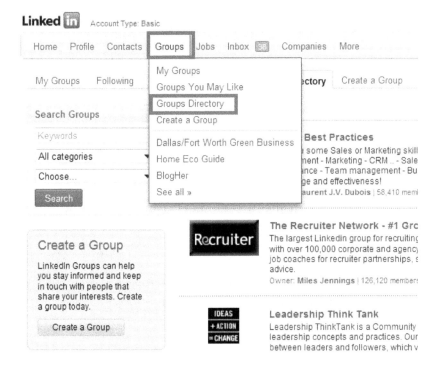

- Search for the groups that align with your interests and join them.
- The drop-down menu options also include:
  - My Groups
  - Following (the groups you've joined)
  - Create Group
  - And a list of the Groups you already belong to

Groups are an excellent resource to tap into other professionals' minds and get their feedback on a question you may have. You'll be amazed at how people are willing to give you their feedback, expertise, and advice.

7. **Post jobs**.
- To post jobs, choose the "Jobs" menu option and select "Post a

Job" from the drop-down menu.

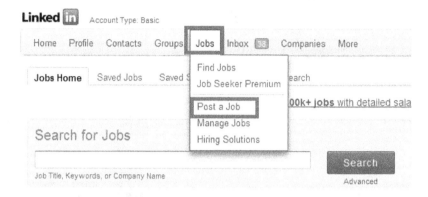

- The drop-down menu options also include to find jobs, and manage your job listings.

8. **Post events**.
   - To post events, go to the "More" menu option and select "Events" from the drop-down menu.

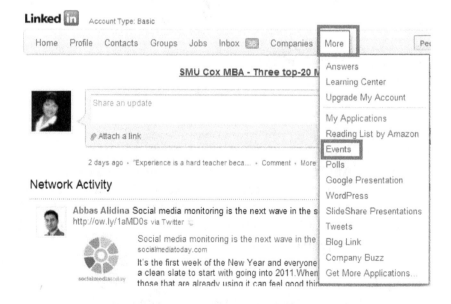

- You can post and join events.

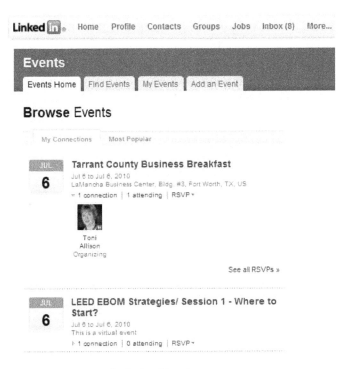

9. **Tap into the power of LinkedIn Answers.**
   - Access LinkedIn "Answers" from the "More" menu option.

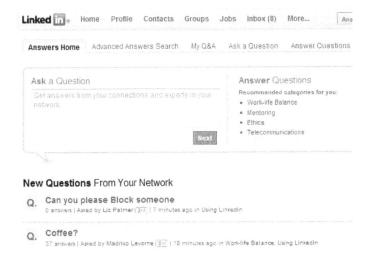

- Observe the open questions.
- Post some answers if you'd like.
- Once you have your file complete and have a few people added to your profile, try posting a question. You'll be surprised as to how many people are willing to share their piece of mind that can provide you with opinions, ideas, and immediate solutions you need.

10. **Combine other applications**.
   - Take advantage of adding other applications to enrich your profile.
   - At minimum install the following:
      o **WordPress**. LinkedIn will link your blog and display your most recent posts.
      o **Tweets**. Lets you manage your Twitter account from within LinkedIn and have the option to share your Tweet on your LinkedIn activity as well. This will help keep both your Twitter and LinkedIn accounts up to date.

EPILOGUE

Social media offers lots of opportunities, but it can seem overwhelming. Keep in mind that social media is also fairly new and even the top marketers are still learning new strategies offered by these new technologies. Don't feel that you're way behind or too late. The fact that you've read this book puts you a step ahead of thousands of other professionals. So don't be afraid to try different approaches and find out what works for you and your audience. Once you have found what works, stick to it and you'll soon become a master of it.

You have in your hands the strategies, tips, additional resources, and step-by-step guidelines to get you started on or enhance your social media marketing program. You have become acquainted with the importance of having and managing your social media presence. As a social media consultant, speaker and trainer, I have observed how the information I've shared has helped entrepreneurs and small businesses find success in using these tools. Once they understood how vital it is for them to take action, they did! And once they learned how to play the social media game, it became easier for them to manage and experience positive results.

After reading this guide, I'm sure that you'll have questions as you plan to incorporate social media into your marketing mix. Don't feel alone. Email me your questions directly at *dina@socialexecs.com* and I'll be sure to reply to your inquiries. You can also submit your questions and search for answers in my forum at *http://www.socialmedia911book.com/forum*.

Are we following each other? Let's stay connected on Twitter

@dinalima1, on Facebook at *http://www.facebook.com/dinalimaspeaker*, and on LinkedIn at *http://www.linnkedin.com/in/dinalima*.

I invite you to check out my Facebook business page where you can glean some tips and observe the diverse informative tabs I've added to maximize my use of this great tool, *http://www.facebook.com/dinalimaspeaker*. Feel free to submit any Facebook questions you may have and I'll be happy to provide you the best information to help you meet your goals.

Contact me for answers to your questions on:

- Social media networking tools such as Twitter, Facebook, and LinkedIn.

- Content management using WordPress.

- Search engine optimization.

Wow! Who would have ever thought that terms such as tweetering, tweets, blogging, and Google as in the action verb "to google" would become part of our everyday English language! The term "Google" was added as a verb in the Oxford English Dictionary in 2006 only five years after it was introduced in 2001.[1, 2] I am sure we can look forward to more interesting terms like these in the future. Innovation can be fun, but also whacky!

Take advantage of the social media marketing revolution to increase customer engagement and revenue. Best wishes to you and your business!

GLOSSARY

Bit.ly. A URL shortener, Bit.ly is a free application that allows you to shorten URLs. This is especially important to use with Twitter because you can only share your message within a limited number of characters.

Blog. Stands for "web log". A blog is a diary-style site where the blogger or author shares information he/she finds interesting, such as articles, videos, commentaries, and the like.

Blog (verb). "To blog" means to author entries or blog posts on your blog site.

Blog Post. An entry, comment, or article written on a weblog.

Blogger. The author or writer of blog posts.

Blogging Platforms and Technologies. Blogging tools such as WordPress are free open source systems widely used around the globe, which are supported and updated by programmers worldwide. Blogging platforms give users the keys to manage their own content. These tools display your entries in reverse chronological order and allow you to update your content easily.

Bounce Rate. Is a term used in website traffic analysis. It represents the percentage of initial visitors to a site who "bounce" away to a different site, rather than continue on to other pages within the same site.

Content Management System (CMS). A CMS is a blogging tool that enables you to manage your blog's content. Some of the most popular CMS tools are Joomla, Drupal and Mambo. WordPress started as a blogging tool but it has now evolved into a full CMS system due to the many different programs called Plugins that enhance the functionality of a blog site. If you want to develop an e-commerce site, Joomla is a very powerful tool with more capabilities to support more complex websites.

Entry. A blog post.

Facebook. Is a free social networking website that allows you to socialize and connect with friends, relatives, employees, business associates and clients. According to Facebook, it has over 500 million active users with thousands of local businesses that have active pages, which has produced over 5.3 billion fans. Many local businesses are enjoying sweet success with Facebook fan page marketing, and you can too.

Flickr. Is a free social networking website used for online photo management and sharing.

LinkedIn. Is a free social networking website for you to share and connect with other business professionals. Successful business owners of the 21st century are LinkedIn.

Micro-Blog. Is a form of multimedia blogging that allows users to send brief updates. One great example is Twitter, which gives you a limited number of characters to express what's happening now.

Open Source. The practice of production and development of online tools that allows access to the source code for enhancements. CMS's are open source technologies that allows programmers around the world to enhance the tools' source code. For example, WordPress is licensed under the GPL license for free use.

Opt-in Email. When you give people the option to receive a "bulk" e-mail, such as a monthly e-newsletter. Unsolicited e-mails are considered a spam.

Retweet. To share another user's message on Twitter.

RSS. Stands for "Really Simple Syndication." It is a family of web feed formats used to publish frequently updated works, such as your blog posts, audio and video. A great example is Google's RSS Feed Burner, *http://feedburner.google.com.*

RSS Feeds. Is a free application that allows you to distribute content to your subscribers regularly and automatically. RSS Feeds sends your updates via a web portal or email each time it detects a new entry on your site.

Search Engine. Is a computer program that allows you to retrieve information online such as Google.

Search Engine Optimization (SEO). Is the process of improving the volume or quality of traffic to your website by the search engines. This can be done via paid or un-paid (natural, organic) search results. There are "on-page" and "off-page" techniques that help increase your organic search rankings.

Search Engine Results Page (SERP). Is the listing of pages returned by the search engine in response to your keyword or query.

Social Media (SM). Is a set of internet- and mobile-based tools for sharing and discussing information among people. It is available 24/7/365, costs you nada (only time), and it is rocking the business world! Networking sites such as Facebook and Twitter are social media tools mostly used for socialization and connecting friends, relatives, and employees.

Social Media Marketing (SMM). Refers to the use of social networks, online communities, blogs, wikis or any other online collaborative media for marketing, sales, public relations and customer service. Some examples of the most popular social media marketing tools are Facebook, Twitter, LinkedIn, Flickr and YouTube.

Social Media Optimization (SMO). Refers to the use of social media tools and technologies to attract visitors to your blog, personal or company website.

Traffic Management Application Tool. Allows you to manage your website traffic providing you specific information such as number of visits to your site, average time visitors spend on your site, bounce rate, the location where your visitors are from. A great example of a tool that enables you to manage your website traffic is Google Analytics.

Tweet. A message that you post or read on Twitter.

TweetDeck. Is a free application for Twitter that allows you to organize, update and manage all your replies, direct messages and retweets.

Twellow. Is a free directory of public Twitter accounts that eases your search for people with whom you want to connect.

Twitter. Is a free social networking website dedicated to micro-blogging that gives you only 140 characters to share what's happening now. It asks you one question: "what's happening" and makes the answer spread across the globe to millions instantly. Experts say that Twitter is the fastest growing social media community site.

Twittering. Is the act of posting a tweet on Twitter.

YouTube. Is your free online video sharing platform.

NOTES

PREFACE

1. Hepburn, Aden. "Facebook: Facts & Figures For 2010," www.digitalbuzzlog.com, March 22, 2010, http://www.digitalbuzzblog.com/facebook-statistics-facts-figures-for-2010/.
2. Weil, Kevin. "Measuring Tweets," www.blog.twitter.com, February 22, 2010, http://blog.twitter.com/2010/02/measuring-tweets.html.
3. Stelzner, Michael A. "2010 Social Media Marketing Industry Report: How Marketers are Using Social Media to Grow Their Business," www.socialmediaexaminer.com, April 2010, http://www.socialmediaexaminer.com/social-media-marketing-industry-report-2010.
4. Camahort Page, Elisa. "The BlogHer –iVillage 2010 Social Media Matters Study," www.blogher.com, http://www.blogher.com/files/Social_Media_Matters_2010.pdf.

INTRODUCTION

1. Green Peace. "What's Behind BP's Logo," www.greenpeace.org.uk, http://www.greenpeace.org.uk/files/tarsands/index.html
2. Flickr. "Behind the Logo," www.flickr.com, http://www.flickr.com/photos/greenpeaceuk/sets/72157623796911855
3. NielsenWire. "Global Advertising: Consumers Trust Real Friends and Virtual Strangers the Most," www.blog.nielsen.com, July 7, 2009, http://blog.nielsen.com/nielsenwire/consumer/global-advertising-consumers-trust-real-friends-and-virtual-strangers-the-most.
4. eMarketer Digital Intelligence. "US Ad Spending: Online Outshines Other Media," www.emarketer.com, December 2010, http://www.emarketer.com/Reports/All/Emarketer_2000725.aspx.
5. Herzog, Ari. "Key Quotes on New Marketing and Social Media,"

www.ariwriter.com, http://ariwriter.com/key-quotes-on-new-marketing-and-social-media.

6.   Social Media Influence. "eBook Review: The Social Contract with Customers," submitted by Matthew Yeomans, March 9, 2010, www.socialmediainfluence.com, http://socialmediainfluence.com/2010/03/09/ebook-review-the-social-contract-with-customers.

7.   CBS News 60 Minutes. "Mark Zuckerberg & Facebook, Part 1," www.cbsnews.com, December 5, 2010, http://www.cbsnews.com/video/watch/?id=7120522n&tag=contentBody;housing.

CHAPTER 1 – THE SOCIAL MEDIA ERA

1.   Stelzner, Michael A. "2010 Social Media Marketing Industry Report: How Marketers are Using Social Media to Grow Their Business," www.socialmediaexaminer.com, April 2010, http://www.socialmediaexaminer.com/social-media-marketing-industry-report-2010.

2.   MarketingProfs. "Small Business Marketing in 2010: A Forecast," www.marketingprofs.com, December 16, 2009, http://www.marketingprofs.com/charts/2009/3258/small-business-marketing-in-2010-a-forecast.

3.   ISITE Design. "2010 Web Strategy Report," www.isitedesign.com, http://www.isitedesign.com/sites/default/files/2010%20Web%20Strategy%20Report.pdf, page 13.

4.   Schonfeld, Erick. "Nearly 75 Million People Visited Twitter's Site In January (comScore)," www.techcrunch.com, February 16, 2010, http://techcrunch.com/2010/02/16/twitter-75-million-people-january.

5.   Weil, Kevin. "Measuring Tweets," www.blog.twitter.com, February 22, 2010, http://blog.twitter.com/2010/02/measuring-tweets.html.

6.   Hepburn, Aden. "Facebook: Facts & Figures For 2010," www.digitalbuzzlog.com, March 22, 2010, http://www.digitalbuzzblog.com/facebook-statistics-facts-figures-for-2010.

7.   LinkedIn. "About Us" page, http://press.linkedin.com.

8.   Camahort Page, Elisa. "The BlogHer –iVillage 2010 Social Media Matters Study," www.blogher.com, http://www.blogher.com/files/Social_Media_Matters_2010.pdf

9.   Corbett, Peter. "Facebook Demographics and Statistics Report 2010 – 145% Growth in 1 Year," www.istrategylabs.com, January 4, 2010, http://www.istrategylabs.com/2010/01/facebook-demographics-and-statistics-report-2010-145-growth-in-1-year.

10. eMarketer Digital Intelligence. "Baby Boomers Get Connected with Social Media," www.emarketer.com, http://www.emarketer.com/Article.aspx?R=1007484.

CHAPTER 2 – THE SIX STEP STRATEGY

1.   Rice, Allison. "10 Ways For Builders to Improve Their Online Marketing Efforts," www.builderonline.com, April 26, 2010, http://www.builderonline.com/marketing/10-ways-for-builders-to-improve-their-online-marketing-efforts.aspx

CHAPTER 4 – THE WEB 2.0 ADVANTAGE

1.   WordPress. "About WordPress," http://wordpress.org/about.
2.   Joomla. "What is Joomla?" http://www.joomla.org/about-joomla.html.

CHAPTER 5 – BLOGGING BASICS

1.   Camahort Page, Elisa. "The BlogHer –iVillage 2010 Social Media Matters Study," www.blogher.com, http://www.blogher.com/files/Social_Media_Matters_2010.pdf.

2.   NielsenWire. "Global Advertising: Consumers Trust Real Friends and Virtual Strangers the Most," www.blog.nielsen.com, July 7, 2009, http://blog.nielsen.com/nielsenwire/consumer/global-advertising-consumers-trust-real-friends-and-virtual-strangers-the-most.

3.   eMarketer Digital Intelligence. "Steady Gains in Blogging for Marketers," www.emarketer.com, August 17, 2010, http://www.emarketer.com/Article.aspx?R=1007871.

4.   eMarketer Digital Intelligence. "The Blogosphere: Colliding with Social and Mainstream Media," www.emarketer.com, September 2010, http://www.emarketer.com/Report.aspx?code=emarketer_2000708.

5.   Weil, Debbie. "Social Media Insights Blog: What's the Call to Action on Your Blog?," www.debbieweil.com, http://www.debbieweil.com/blog/whats-the-call-to-action-on-your-blog.

CHAPTER 7 – TOOLS OF THE TRADE

1. ReadWriteWeb. "Analysis: What are the Web's Top Sources of Referral Traffic?," www.readwriteweb.com, July 28, 2010, http://www.readwriteweb.com/archives/analysis_what_are_the_webs_top_sources_of_referral_traffic.php
2. Mashable. "The Web in Numbers: the Rise of Social Media," www.mashable.com, http://mashable.com/2009/04/17/web-in-numbers-social-media
3. Google Press Center. "Google To Acquire YouTube for $1.65 Billion in Stock," www.google.com, http://www.google.com/intl/en/press/pressrel/google_youtube.html
4. MSNBC. "Google buys YouTube for $1.65 billion," www.msnbc.com, http://www.msnbc.msn.com/id/15196982
5. Flickr's blog. ""5,000,000,000" www.blog.flickr.net, http://blog.flickr.net/en/2010/09/19/5000000000

CHAPTER 9 – TWITTER: ATTRACT LOYAL FOLLOWERS

1. Gaudin, Sharon. "Twitter now has 75M users; most asleep at the mouse," www.computerworld.com, January 26, 2010, http://www.computerworld.com/s/article/9148878/Twitter_now_has_75M_users_most_asleep_at_the_mouse

EPILOGUE

1. Search Engine Watch. "Google Now A Verb In The Oxford English Dictionary," www.searchenginewatch.com, http://blog.searchenginewatch.com/060629-105413
2. Merriam Webster online dictionary. Definition of "google." http://www.merriam-webster.com/dictionary/google

Find social media tips and answers at
www.SocialMedia911Book.com

Let's Connect!

www.facebook.com/dinalimaspeaker

www.twitter.com/dinalima1

www.linkedin.com/in/dinalima

For Social Media and Web/Blog Design Services

Visit www.SocialExecs.com

Contact Dina@SocialExecs.com

Social Media Integration and Management

Search Engine Optimization (SEO)

Optimized Website and Blog Design

www.ingramcontent.com/pod-product-compliance
Lightning Source LLC
Chambersburg PA
CBHW071149050326
40689CB00011B/2038